INTRODUCTION

In today's society, we are under so much stress and every one of us is dealing with something. Every single person has issues to deal with and we can often feel lonely and isolated in our problems.

Luckily, we're not alone.

The bible is full of promises made by God for nearly every situation that you find yourself in. According to some accounts, there are over 8,000 promises made by God in the bible.

The best part?

What God promised, He will deliver. His promises never fail.

When it comes to the promises He made, the problem most of us have is timing and belief, both of which are essential to realizing the promises made to us.

God has a plan and everything happens according to that plan. We may not always understand why certain things are happening in our lives, but most often when we look back, it's easy to connect the dots and see why and how we got to where we are.

One of the most important things we need to keep in mind is that God doesn't work on our schedule. He works on his own timeline and often, what we are praying and believing for isn't happening as quickly as we would like. We need to have patience.

We also need to have faith that God is working for us and for our good. Without faith, God's promises often remain unfulfilled. We must mix faith with expectancy while we are being patient for God to fulfill His promises.

So how do we use the promises of God to get what we ask for?

It's actually very simple.

First, ask for what you want.

Then let it go, knowing that what you have asked for is on its way. Expect it to come. Have faith that God heard you and is working in the unseen realm to help you with what you have asked for.

It's that simple.

This book is full of God's promises organized into chapters that deal with specific issues. Some of the promises are repeated in multiple chapters, as

WHAT GOD PROMISED

Over 500 Promises From The New
International Version of the Bible

Chris Cavanagh

CONTENTS

they apply to a variety of topics. All of the verses are taken from the New International Version of the bible, so each is written in friendly, easy to understand language.

I hope you enjoy this book and it helps inspire you to realize your best life.

God bless you.

> "I am with you and will watch over you wherever you go, and I will bring you back to this land. I will not leave you until I have done what I have promised you." (Genesis 28:15)

PROMISES FOR
WHEN YOU PRAY

Then the Lord said to Abraham, "Why did Sarah laugh and say, 'Will I really have a child, now that I am old?' Is anything too hard for the Lord? I will return to you at the appointed time next year, and Sarah will have a son." (Genesis 18:13-14)

"Ah, Sovereign Lord, you have made the heavens and the earth by your great power and outstretched arm. Nothing is too hard for you." (Jeremiah 32:17)

"I am the Lord, the God of all mankind. Is anything too hard for me?" (Jeremiah 32:27)

"Ask and it will be given to you; seek and you will find; knock and the door will be opened to you. For everyone who asks receives; the one who seeks finds; and to the one who knocks, the door will be opened."

"Which of you, if your son asks for bread, will give him a stone? Or if he asks for a fish, will give him a snake? If you, then, though you are evil, know how to give good gifts to your children, how much more will your Father in heaven give good gifts to those who ask him!" (Matthew 7:7-11)

Therefore I tell you, whatever you ask for in prayer, believe that you have received it, and it will be yours. (Mark 11:24)

"Even Elizabeth, your relative is going to have a

child in her old age, and she who was said to be unable to conceive is in her sixth month. For no word from God will ever fail." (Luke 1:36-37)

"And will not God bring about justice for his chosen ones, who cry out to him day and night? Will he keep putting them off? I tell you, he will see that they get justice, and quickly. However, when the Son of Man comes, will he find faith on the earth?" (Luke 18:7-8)

And I will do whatever you ask in my name, so that the Father may be glorified in the Son. You may ask me for anything in my name, and I will do it. (John 14:13-14)

In that day you will no longer ask me anything. Very truly I tell you, my Father will give you whatever you ask in my name. Until now you have not asked for anything in my name. Ask and you will receive, and your joy will be complete. (John 16:23-24)

He who did not spare his own Son, but gave him up for us all—how will he not also, along with him, graciously give us all things? (Romans 8:32)

Now to him who is able to do immeasurably more than all we ask or imagine, according to his power that is at work within us, to him be glory in the church and in Christ Jesus throughout all generations, for ever and ever! Amen. (Ephesians 3:20-21)

Therefore, since we have a great high priest who has ascended into heaven, Jesus the Son of God, let us hold firmly to the faith we profess. For we do not have a high priest who is unable to empathize with our weaknesses, but we have one who has been tempted in every way, just as we are—yet he did not sin. Let us then approach God's throne of grace with confidence, so that we may receive mercy and find grace to help us in our time of need. (Hebrews 4:14-16)

This is the confidence we have in approaching God: that if we ask anything according to his will, he hears us. And if we know that he hears us—whatever we ask—we know that we have what we asked of him. (1 John 5:14-15)

ANSWERED PRAYER

I waited patiently for the Lord; he turned
to me and heard my cry. (Psalm 40:1)

Praise be to God, who has not rejected my prayer
or withheld his love from me! (Psalm 66:20)

If anyone turns a deaf ear to my instruction, even
their prayers are detestable. (Proverbs 28:9)

Before they call I will answer; while they are
still speaking I will hear. (Isaiah 65:24)

"Ask and it will be given to you; seek and you will
find; knock and the door will be opened to you. For
everyone who asks receives; the one who seeks finds;
and to the one who knocks, the door will be opened.

Then you will call on me and come and pray to me, and
I will listen to you. You will seek me and find me when
you seek me with all your heart." (Jeremiah 29:12-13)

'Call to me and I will answer you and tell
you great and unsearchable things you
do not know.' (Jeremiah 33:3)

"Which of you, if your son asks for bread, will
give him a stone? Or if he asks for a fish, will give
him a snake? If you, then, though you are evil,

know how to give good gifts to your children, how much more will your Father in heaven give good gifts to those who ask him!" (Matthew 7:7-11)

Jesus replied, "Truly I tell you, if you have faith and do not doubt, not only can you do what was done to the fig tree, but also you can say to this mountain, 'Go, throw yourself into the sea,' and it will be done. If you believe, you will receive whatever you ask for in prayer." (Matthew 21:21-22)

"Have faith in God," Jesus answered. "Truly I tell you, if anyone says to this mountain, 'Go, throw yourself into the sea,' and does not doubt in their heart but believes that what they say will happen, it will be done for them. Therefore I tell you, whatever you ask for in prayer, believe that you have received it, and it will be yours." (Mark 11:22-24)

We know that God does not listen to sinners. He listens to the godly person who does his will. (John 9:31)

And I will do whatever you ask in my name, so that the Father may be glorified in the Son. You may ask me for anything in my name, and I will do it. (John 14:13-14)

If you remain in me and my words remain in you, ask whatever you wish, and it will be done for you. (John 15:7)

In that day you will no longer ask me anything. Very truly I tell you, my Father will give you whatever you ask in my name. Until now you have not asked for anything in my name. Ask and you will receive, and your joy will be complete. (John 16:23-24)

Do not be anxious about anything, but in every situation, by prayer and petition, with thanksgiving, present your requests to God. (Philippians 4:6)

Therefore confess your sins to each other and pray for each other so that you may be healed. The prayer of a righteous person is powerful and effective. Elijah was a human being, even as we are. He prayed earnestly that it would not rain, and it did not rain on the land for three and a half years. (James 5:16-17)

For the eyes of the Lord are on the righteous and his ears are attentive to their prayer, but the face of the Lord is against those who do evil. (1 Peter 3:12)

And receive from him anything we ask, because we keep his commands and do what pleases him. (1 John 3:22)

This is the confidence we have in approaching God: that if we ask anything according to his will, he hears us. And if we know that he hears us—whatever we ask—we know that we have what we asked of him. (1 John 5:14-15)

ASSURANCE

Even though I walk through the darkest valley,
I will fear no evil, for you are with me; your rod
and your staff, they comfort me. (Psalm 23:4)

The fruit of that righteousness will be
peace; its effect will be quietness and
confidence forever. (Isaiah 32:17)

Very truly I tell you, whoever hears my word
and believes him who sent me has eternal
life and will not be judged but has crossed
over from death to life. (John 5:24)

Very truly I tell you, the one who believes
has eternal life. (John 6:47)

My sheep listen to my voice; I know them, and
they follow me. I give them eternal life, and they
shall never perish; no one will snatch them out
of my hand. My Father, who has given them to
me, is greater than all; no one can snatch them
out of my Father's hand. (John 10:27-29)

Therefore, since we have been justified through
faith, we have peace with God through our
Lord Jesus Christ. (Romans 5:1)

And hope does not put us to shame, because God's
love has been poured out into our hearts through the

Holy Spirit, who has been given to us. (Romans 5:5)

For those who are led by the Spirit of God are the children of God. The Spirit you received does not make you slaves, so that you live in fear again; rather, the Spirit you received brought about your adoption to sonship. And by him we cry, "*Abba,* Father." The Spirit himself testifies with our spirit that we are God's children. Now if we are children, then we are heirs—heirs of God and co-heirs with Christ, if indeed we share in his sufferings in order that we may also share in his glory. (Romans 8:14-17)

For I am convinced that neither death nor life, neither angels nor demons, neither the present nor the future, nor any powers, neither height nor depth, nor anything else in all creation, will be able to separate us from the love of God that is in Christ Jesus our Lord. (Romans 8:38-39)

Therefore we do not lose heart. Though outwardly we are wasting away, yet inwardly we are being renewed day by day. For our light and momentary troubles are achieving for us an eternal glory that far outweighs them all. So we fix our eyes not on what is seen, but on what is unseen, since what is seen is temporary, but what is unseen is eternal. (2 Corinthians 4:16-18)

For it is by grace you have been saved, through faith—and this is not from yourselves, it is the gift of God. (Ephesians 2:8)

In him and through faith in him we may approach God with freedom and confidence. (Ephesians 3:12)

My goal is that they may be encouraged in heart and united in love, so that they may have the full riches of complete understanding, in order that they may know the mystery of God, namely, Christ. (Colossians 2:2)

That is why I am suffering as I am. Yet this is no cause for shame, because I know whom I have believed, and am convinced that he is able to guard what I have entrusted to him until that day. (2 Timothy 1:12)

We want each of you to show this same diligence to the very end, so that what you hope for may be fully realized. (Hebrews 6:11)

Let us draw near to God with a sincere heart and with the full assurance that faith brings, having our hearts sprinkled to cleanse us from a guilty conscience and having our bodies washed with pure water. (Hebrews 10:22)

Now faith is confidence in what we hope for and assurance about what we do not see. (Hebrews 11:1)

And this is what he promised us— eternal life. (1 John 2:25)

Dear friends, now we are children of God, and what we will be has not yet been made known. But we know that when Christ appears, we shall be like him, for we shall see him as he is. (1 John 3:2)

We know that we have passed from death to life, because we love each other. Anyone who does not love remains in death. (1 John 3:14)

And this is the testimony: God has given us eternal life, and this life is in his Son. Whoever has the Son has life; whoever does not have the Son of God does not have life.I write these things to you who believe in the name of the Son of God so that you may know that you have eternal life. (1 John 5:11-13)

CONFIDENCE

The eternal God is your refuge, and underneath are the everlasting arms. He will drive out your enemies before you, saying, 'Destroy them!' (Deuteronomy 33:27)

"Have I not commanded you? Be strong and courageous. Do not be afraid; do not be discouraged, for the Lord your God will be with you wherever you go." (Joshua 1:9)

When all our enemies heard about this, all the surrounding nations were afraid and lost their self-confidence, because they realized that this work had been done with the help of our God. (Nehemiah 6:16)

With him is only the arm of flesh, but with us is the Lord our God to help us and to fight our battles." And the people gained confidence from what Hezekiah the king of Judah said. (2 Chronicles 32:8)

With your help I can advance against a troop; with my God I can scale a wall. (Psalm 18:29)

It is God who arms me with strength and keeps my way secure. He makes my feet like the feet of a deer; he causes me to stand on the heights. (Psalm 18:32-33)

Some trust in chariots and some in horses, but we trust in the name of the Lord our God. (Psalm 20:7)

The Lord is my strength and my shield; my heart trusts in him, and he helps me. My heart leaps for joy, and with my song I praise him. (Psalm 28:7)

For you created my inmost being; you knit me together in my mother's womb. I praise you because I am fearfully and wonderfully made; your works are wonderful, I know that full well. (Psalm 139:13-14)

For the Lord will be at your side and will keep your foot from being snared. (Proverbs 3:26)

The fruit of that righteousness will be peace; its effect will be quietness and confidence forever. (Isaiah 32:17)

But those who hope in the Lord will renew their strength. They will soar on wings like eagles; they will run and not grow weary, they will walk and not be faint. (Isaiah 40:31)

So do not fear, for I am with you; do not be dismayed, for I am your God. I will strengthen you and help you; I will uphold you with my righteous right hand. (Isaiah 41:10)

"But blessed is the one who trusts in the Lord, whose confidence is in him." (Jeremiah 17:7)

The Sovereign Lord is my strength; he makes my feet like the feet of a deer, he enables me to tread on the heights. For the director of music. On my stringed instruments. (Habakkuk 3:19)

I came to you in weakness with great fear and trembling. My message and my preaching were not with wise and persuasive words, but with a demonstration of the Spirit's power, so that your faith might not rest on human wisdom, but on God's power. (1 Corinthians 2:3-5)

Are we beginning to commend ourselves again? Or do we need, like some people, letters of recommendation to you or from you? You yourselves are our letter, written on our hearts, known and read by everyone. You show that you are a letter from Christ, the result of our ministry, written not with ink but with the Spirit of the living God, not on tablets of stone but on tablets of human hearts. (2 Corinthians 3:1-4)

But he said to me, "My grace is sufficient for you, for my power is made perfect in weakness." Therefore I will boast all the more gladly about my weaknesses, so that Christ's power may rest on me. That is why, for Christ's sake, I delight in weaknesses, in insults, in hardships, in persecutions, in difficulties. For when I am weak, then I am strong. (2 Corinthians 12:9-10)

In him and through faith in him we may approach God with freedom and confidence. (Ephesians 3:12)

Being confident of this, that he who began a good work in you will carry it on to completion until the day of Christ Jesus. (Philippians 1:6)

I can do all this through Him who gives me strength. (Philippians 4:13)

For the Spirit God gave us does not make us timid, but gives us power, love and self-discipline. (2 Timothy 1:7)

Let us then approach God's throne of grace with confidence, so that we may receive mercy and find grace to help us in our time of need. (Hebrews 4:16)

So do not throw away your confidence; it will be richly rewarded. You need to persevere so that when you have done the will of God, you will receive what he has promised. (Hebrews 10:35-36)

So we say with confidence, "The Lord is my helper; I will not be afraid. What can mere mortals do to me?" (Hebrews 13:6)

This is how love is made complete among us so that
we will have confidence on the day of judgment:
In this world we are like Jesus. (1 John 4:17)

This is the confidence we have in approaching
God: that if we ask anything according to
his will, he hears us. (1 John 5:14)

DEPRESSION

The Lord himself goes before you and will be with you; he will never leave you nor forsake you. Do not be afraid; do not be discouraged. (Deuteronomy 31:8)

Answer me when I call to you, my righteous God. Give me relief from my distress; have mercy on me and hear my prayer. (Psalm 4:1)

Fill my heart with joy when their grain and new wine abound. (Psalm 4:7)

Even though I walk through the darkest valley, I will fear no evil, for you are with me; your rod and your staff, they comfort me. (Psalm 23:4)

Be strong and take heart, all you who hope in the Lord. (Psalm 31:24)

The Lord is close to the brokenhearted and saves those who are crushed in spirit. (Psalm 34:18)

The Lord makes firm the steps of the one who delights in him; though he may stumble, he will not fall, for the Lord upholds him with his hand. (Psalm 37:23-24)

I waited patiently for the Lord; he turned to me and heard my cry. He lifted me out of the slimy pit, out of the mud and mire; he set my feet on a rock and gave me a firm place to stand. (Psalm 40:1-2)

My soul is downcast within me; therefore I will
remember you from the land of the Jordan, the
heights of Hermon—from Mount Mizar. Deep calls
to deep in the roar of your waterfalls; all your waves
and breakers have swept over me. By day the Lord
directs his love, at night his song is with me—a
prayer to the God of my life. I say to God my Rock,
"Why have you forgotten me? Why must I go about
mourning, oppressed by the enemy?" My bones
suffer mortal agony as my foes taunt me, saying to
me all day long, "Where is your God?" Why, my soul,
are you downcast? Why so disturbed within me? Put
your hope in God, for I will yet praise him,
my Savior and my God. (Psalm 42:6-11)

Your righteousness, God, reaches to the heavens,
you who have done great things. Who is like you,
God? Though you have made me see troubles,
many and bitter, you will restore my life again;
from the depths of the earth you will again
bring me up. You will increase my honor and
comfort me once more. (Psalm 71:19-21)

Trust in the Lord with all your heart and
lean not on your own understanding; in all
your ways submit to him, and he will make
your paths straight. (Proverbs 3:5-6)

So do not fear, for I am with you; do not be
dismayed, for I am your God. I will strengthen
you and help you; I will uphold you with my
righteous right hand. (Isaiah 41:10)

For I know the plans I have for you," declares the Lord,
"plans to prosper you and not to harm you, plans
to give you hope and a future. (Jeremiah 29:11)

I say to myself, "The Lord is my portion; therefore I will wait for him." (Lamentations 3:24)

Come to me, all you who are weary and burdened, and I will give you rest. (Matthew 11:28)

"I have told you these things, so that in me you may have peace. In this world you will have trouble. But take heart! I have overcome the world." (John 16:33)

For I am convinced that neither death nor life, neither angels nor demons, neither the present nor the future, nor any powers, neither height nor depth, nor anything else in all creation, will be able to separate us from the love of God that is in Christ Jesus our Lord. (Romans 8:38-39)

Praise be to the God and Father of our Lord Jesus Christ, the Father of compassion and the God of all comfort, who comforts us in all our troubles, so that we can comfort those in any trouble with the comfort we ourselves receive from God. (2 Corinthians 1:3-4)

Finally, brothers and sisters, whatever is true, whatever is noble, whatever is right, whatever is pure, whatever is lovely, whatever is admirable —if anything is excellent or praiseworthy— think about such things. (Philippians 4:8)

I can do all this through Him who gives me strength. (Philippians 4:13)

Cast all your anxiety on him because he cares for you. (1 Peter 5:7)

DISTRESS

I am with you and will watch over you wherever
you go, and I will bring you back to this land.
I will not leave you until I have done what I
have promised you. (Genesis 28:15)

But if from there you seek the Lord your God, you will
find him if you seek him with all your heart and with all
your soul. When you are in distress and all these things
have happened to you, then in later days you will return
to the Lord your God and obey him. For the Lord your
God is a merciful God; he will not abandon or destroy
you or forget the covenant with your ancestors, which
he confirmed to them by oath. (Deuteronomy 4:29-31)

The Lord himself goes before you and will be with
you; he will never leave you nor forsake you. Do not be
afraid; do not be discouraged. (Deuteronomy 31:8)

Look to the Lord and his strength; seek his
face always. (1 Chronicles 16:11)

Answer me when I call to you, my righteous
God. Give me relief from my distress; have mercy
on me and hear my prayer. (Psalm 4:1)

The Lord is a refuge for the oppressed, a stronghold
in times of trouble. Those who know your name
trust in you, for you, Lord, have never forsaken
those who seek you. (Psalm 9:9-10)

In my distress I called to the Lord; I cried to my God for help. From his temple he heard my voice; my cry came before him, into his ears. (Psalm 18:6)

The Lord is my strength and my shield; my heart trusts in him, and he helps me. My heart leaps for joy, and with my song I praise him. (Psalm 28:7)

I sought the Lord, and he answered me; he delivered me from all my fears. Those who look to him are radiant; their faces are never covered with shame. (Psalm 34:4-5)

The Lord is my strength and my shield; my heart trusts in him, and he helps me. My heart leaps for joy, and with my song I praise him. (Psalm 42:5-6)

Have mercy on me, my God, have mercy on me, for in you I take refuge. I will take refuge in the shadow of your wings until the disaster has passed. (Psalm 57:1)

From the ends of the earth I call to you, I call as my heart grows faint; lead me to the rock that is higher than I. (Psalm 61:2)

Yet I am always with you; you hold me by my right hand. (Psalm 73:23)

My flesh and my heart may fail, but God is the strength of my heart and my portion forever. (Psalm 73:26)

Then they cried out to the Lord in their trouble, and he delivered them from their distress. (Psalm 107:6)

When hard pressed, I cried to the Lord;
He brought me into a spacious place.
(Psalm 118:5)

I call on the Lord in my distress, and
he answers me. (Psalm 120:1)

You will keep in perfect peace those whose minds are steadfast, because they trust in you. (Isaiah 26:3)

So do not fear, for I am with you; do not be dismayed, for I am your God. I will strengthen you and help you; I will uphold you with my righteous right hand. (Isaiah 41:10)

Because of the Lord's great love we are not consumed, for his compassions never fail. They are new every morning; great is your faithfulness. I say to myself, "The Lord is my portion; therefore I will wait for him." (Lamentations 3:22-24)

Therefore do not worry about tomorrow, for tomorrow will worry about itself. Each day has enough trouble of its own. (Matthew 6:34)

Are not five sparrows sold for two pennies? Yet not one of them is forgotten by God. Indeed, the very hairs of your head are all numbered. Don't be afraid; you are worth more than many sparrows. (Luke 12:6-7)

Who shall separate us from the love of Christ? Shall trouble or hardship or persecution or famine or nakedness or danger or sword? As it is written:

"For your sake we face death all day long; we are considered as sheep to be slaughtered."

No, in all these things we are more than conquerors through him who loved us. For I am convinced that neither death nor life, neither angels nor demons, neither the present nor the future, nor any powers, neither height nor depth, nor anything else in all creation, will be able to separate us from the love of God that is in Christ Jesus our Lord. (Romans 8:35-39)

We do not want you to be uninformed, brothers and
sisters, about the troubles we experienced in the
province of Asia. We were under great pressure, far
beyond our ability to endure, so that we despaired
of life itself. Indeed, we felt we had received the
sentence of death. But this happened that we might
not rely on ourselves but on God, who raises the dead.
He has delivered us from such a deadly peril, and he
will deliver us again. On him we have set our hope
that he will continue to deliver us, as you help us
by your prayers. Then many will give thanks on our
behalf for the gracious favor granted us in answer
to the prayers of many. (2 Corinthians 1:8-11)

But he said to me, "My grace is sufficient for you, for
my power is made perfect in weakness." Therefore I
will boast all the more gladly about my weaknesses,
so that Christ's power may rest on me. That is why,
for Christ's sake, I delight in weaknesses, in insults, in
hardships, in persecutions, in difficulties. For when I
am weak, then I am strong. (2 Corinthians 12:9-10)

And my God will meet all your needs according to the
riches of his glory in Christ Jesus. To our God and Father
be glory for ever and ever. Amen. (Philippians 4:19-20)

Let us then approach God's throne of grace with
confidence, so that we may receive mercy and find
grace to help us in our time of need. (Hebrews 4:16)

Keep your lives free from the love of money
and be content with what you have, because
God has said, "Never will I leave you; never will
I forsake you." So we say with confidence, "The

Lord is my helper; I will not be afraid. What can mere mortals do to me?" (Hebrews 13:5-6)

Humble yourselves, therefore, under God's mighty hand, that he may lift you up in due time. Cast all your anxiety on him because he cares for you. (1 Peter 5:6-7)

FAITH

Trust in the Lord with all your heart and lean not on your own understanding; in all your ways submit to him, and he will make your paths straight. (Proverbs 3:5-6)

He replied, "Because you have so little faith. Truly I tell you, if you have faith as small as a mustard seed, you can say to this mountain, 'Move from here to there,' and it will move. Nothing will be impossible for you." (Matthew 17:20)

If you believe, you will receive whatever you ask for in prayer. (Matthew 21:22)

"'If you can'?" said Jesus. "Everything is possible for one who believes." (Mark 9:23)

"Have faith in God," Jesus answered. "Truly I tell you, if anyone says to this mountain, 'Go, throw yourself into the sea,' and does not doubt in their heart but believes that what they say will happen, it will be done for them. Therefore I tell you, whatever you ask for in prayer, believe that you have received it, and it will be yours. (Mark 11:22-24)

Then Jesus told him, "Because you have seen me, you have believed; blessed are those who have not seen and yet have believed." (John 20:29)

Consequently, faith comes from hearing the

message, and the message is heard through
the word about Christ. (Romans 10:17)

For it is by grace you have been saved, through faith—
and this is not from yourselves, it is the gift of God— not
by works, so that no one can boast. (Ephesians 2:8-9)

Fight the good fight of the faith. Take hold of
the eternal life to which you were called when
you made your good confession in the presence
of many witnesses. (1 Timothy 6:12)

We want each of you to show this same diligence to
the very end, so that what you hope for may be fully
realized. We do not want you to become lazy, but to
imitate those who through faith and patience inherit
what has been promised. (Hebrews 6:11-12)

Let us hold unswervingly to the hope we profess,
for he who promised is faithful. (Hebrews 10:23)

So do not throw away your confidence; it will be
richly rewarded. You need to persevere so that when
you have done the will of God, you will receive what
he has promised. For, "In just a little while, he who is
coming will come and will not delay." And, "But my
righteous one will live by faith. And I take no pleasure
in the one who shrinks back." (Hebrews 10:35-38)

And without faith it is impossible to please
God, because anyone who comes to him must
believe that he exists and that he rewards
those who earnestly seek him. (Hebrews 11:6)

If any of you lacks wisdom, you should ask God, who
gives generously to all without finding fault, and it will
be given to you. But when you ask, you must believe and
not doubt, because the one who doubts is like a wave of

the sea, blown and tossed by the wind. (James 1:5-6)

Is anyone among you sick? Let them call the elders of the church to pray over them and anoint them with oil in the name of the Lord. And the prayer offered in faith will make the sick person well; the Lord will raise them up. If they have sinned, they will be forgiven. Therefore confess your sins to each other and pray for each other so that you may be healed. The prayer of a righteous person is powerful and effective. Elijah was a human being, even as we are. He prayed earnestly that it would not rain, and it did not rain on the land for three and a half years. (James 5:14-17)

For everyone born of God overcomes the world. This is the victory that has overcome the world, even our faith. (1 John 5:4)

FEAR

Do not be afraid of them; the Lord your God
himself will fight for you. (Deuteronomy 3:22)

Be strong and courageous. Do not be afraid or
terrified because of them, for the Lord your
God goes with you; he will never leave you
nor forsake you. (Deuteronomy 31:6)

Even though I walk through the darkest valley,
I will fear no evil, for you are with me; your rod
and your staff, they comfort me. (Psalm 23:4)

The Lord is my light and my salvation-whom shall I
fear? The Lord is the stronghold of my life—of whom
shall I be afraid? When the wicked advance against
me to devour me, it is my enemies and my foes who
will stumble and fall. Though an army besiege me,
my heart will not fear; though war break out against
me, even then I will be confident. (Psalm 27:1-3)

I sought the Lord, and he answered me; he
delivered me from all my fears. (Psalm 34:4)

God is our refuge and strength, an ever-present help
in trouble. Therefore we will not fear, though the
earth give way and the mountains fall into the heart
of the sea, though its waters roar and foam and the
mountains quake with their surging. (Psalm 46:1–3)

When I am afraid, I put my trust in you. In God, whose

word I praise— in God I trust and am not afraid. What can mere mortals do to me? (Psalm 56:3-4)

Surely God is my salvation; I will trust and not be afraid. The Lord, the Lord himself, is my strength and my defense; he has become my salvation. (Isaiah 12:2)

Say to those with fearful hearts, "Be strong, do not fear; your God will come, he will come with vengeance; with divine retribution he will come to save you." (Isaiah 35:4)

So do not fear, for I am with you; do not be dismayed, for I am your God. I will strengthen you and help you; I will uphold you with my righteous right hand. (Isaiah 41:10)

For I am the Lord your God who takes hold of your right hand and says to you, Do not fear; I will help you. Do not be afraid, you worm Jacob, little Israel, do not fear, for I myself will help you," declares the Lord, your Redeemer, the Holy One of Israel. (Isaiah 41:13-14)

But now, this is what the Lord says—he who created you, Jacob, he who formed you, Israel: "Do not fear, for I have redeemed you; I have summoned you by name; you are mine. (Isaiah 43:1)

"I, even I, am he who comforts you. Who are you that you fear mere mortals, human beings who are but grass, that you forget the Lord your Maker, who stretches out the heavens and who lays the foundations of the earth, that you live in constant terror every day because of the wrath of the oppressor, who is bent on destruction? For where is the wrath of the oppressor? (Isaiah 51:12-13)

Peace I leave with you; my peace I give you. I do not give to you as the world gives. Do not let your hearts be troubled and do not be afraid. (John 14:27)

For the Spirit God gave us does not make us timid, but gives us power, love and self-discipline. (2 Timothy 1:7)

So we say with confidence, "The Lord is my helper; I will not be afraid. What can mere mortals do to me?" (Hebrews 13:6)

There is no fear in love. But perfect love drives out fear, because fear has to do with punishment. The one who fears is not made perfect in love. (1 John 4:18)

When I saw him, I fell at his feet as though dead. Then he placed his right hand on me and said: "Do not be afraid. I am the First and the Last." (Revelation 1:17)

FINANCES

The Lord will grant you abundant prosperity—in the fruit of your womb, the young of your livestock and the crops of your ground—in the land he swore to your ancestors to give you. The Lord will open the heavens, the storehouse of his bounty, to send rain on your land in season and to bless all the work of your hands. You will lend to many nations but will borrow from none. (Deuteronomy 28:11-12)

But remember the Lord your God, for it is he who gives you the ability to produce wealth, and so confirms his covenant, which he swore to your ancestors, as it is today. (Deuteronomy 8:18)

"Submit to God and be at peace with him; in this way prosperity will come to you." (Job 22:21)

Fear the Lord, you his holy people, for those who fear him lack nothing. The lions may grow weak and hungry, but those who seek the Lord lack no good thing. (Psalm 34:9-10)

I was young and now I am old, yet I have never seen the righteous forsaken or their children begging bread. (Psalm 37:25)

Honor the Lord with your wealth, with the firstfruits of all your crops; then your barns will

be filled to overflowing, and your vats will brim
over with new wine. (Proverbs 3:9-10)

The blessing of the Lord brings wealth, without
painful toil for it. (Proverbs 10:22)

I will prevent pests from devouring your crops, and the
vines in your fields will not drop their fruit before it
is ripe," says the Lord Almighty. "Then all the nations
will call you blessed, for yours will be a delightful
land," says the Lord Almighty. (Malachi 3:11-12)

But seek first his kingdom and his righteousness, and all
these things will be given to you as well. (Matthew 6:33)

Give, and it will be given to you. A good measure,
pressed down, shaken together and running over,
will be poured into your lap. For with the measure
you use, it will be measured to you. (Luke 6:38)

The thief comes only to steal and kill and
destroy; I have come that they may have life,
and have it to the full. (John 10:10)

And God is able to bless you abundantly, so that in all
things at all times, having all that you need, you will
abound in every good work. (2 Corinthians 9:8)

And my God will meet all your needs according to the
riches of his glory in Christ Jesus. (Philippians 4:19)

This is the confidence we have in approaching
God: that if we ask anything according to his
will, he hears us. And if we know that he hears
us—whatever we ask—we know that we have
what we asked of him. (1 John 5:14-15)

FORGIVENESS

In accordance with your great love, forgive the sin of these people, just as you have pardoned them from the time they left Egypt until now." The Lord replied, "I have forgiven them, as you asked. Nevertheless, as surely as I live and as surely as the glory of the Lord fills the whole earth." (Numbers 14:19-21)

Whoever conceals their sins does not prosper, but the one who confesses and renounces them finds mercy. (Proverbs 28:13)

"Come now, let us settle the matter," says the Lord. "Though your sins are like scarlet, they shall be as white as snow; though they are red as crimson, they shall be like wool. (Isaiah 1:18)

Then I acknowledged my sin to you and did not cover up my iniquity. I said, "I will confess my transgressions to the Lord." And you forgave the guilt of my sin. (Psalm 32:5)

I have swept away your offenses like a cloud, your sins like the morning mist. Return to me, for I have redeemed you. (Isaiah 44:22)

Let the wicked forsake their ways and the unrighteous their thoughts. Let them turn to the Lord, and he will have mercy on them, and to our

God, for he will freely pardon. (Isaiah 55:7)

No longer will they teach their neighbor, or say to one another, 'Know the Lord,' because they will all know me, from the least of them to the greatest," declares the Lord. "For I will forgive their wickedness and will remember their sins no more." (Jeremiah 31:34)

The Lord our God is merciful and forgiving, even though we have rebelled against him. (Daniel 9:9)

Who is a God like you, who pardons sin and forgives the transgression of the remnant of his inheritance? You do not stay angry forever but delight to show mercy. You will again have compassion on us; you will tread our sins underfoot and hurl all our iniquities into the depths of the sea. (Micah 7:18-19)

For if you forgive other people when they sin against you, your heavenly Father will also forgive you. But if you do not forgive others their sins, your Father will not forgive your sins. (Matthew 6:14-15)

"Do not judge, and you will not be judged. Do not condemn, and you will not be condemned. Forgive, and you will be forgiven." (Luke 6:37)

Repent, then, and turn to God, so that your sins may be wiped out, that times of refreshing may come from the Lord. (Acts 3:19)

In him we have redemption through his blood, the forgiveness of sins, in accordance with the riches of God's grace. (Ephesians 1:7)

Get rid of all bitterness, rage and anger, brawling and slander, along with every form of malice. Be kind and compassionate to one another, forgiving each other, just as in Christ God forgave you. (Ephesians 4:31-32)

For he has rescued us from the dominion of darkness and brought us into the kingdom of the Son he loves, in whom we have redemption, the forgiveness of sins. (Colossians 1:13-14)

For I will forgive their wickedness and will remember their sins no more. (Hebrews 8:12)

Then he adds: "Their sins and lawless acts I will remember no more." (Hebrews 10:17)

Therefore confess your sins to each other and pray for each other so that you may be healed. The prayer of a righteous person is powerful and effective. (James 5:16)

If we confess our sins, he is faithful and just and will forgive us our sins and purify us from all unrighteousness. (1 John 1:9)

FRUITFULNESS

I will make you very fruitful; I will make nations of
you, and kings will come from you. (Genesis 17:6)

"'Follow my decrees and be careful to obey my
laws, and you will live safely in the land. Then the
land will yield its fruit, and you will eat your fill
and live there in safety." (Leviticus 25:18-19)

He will love you and bless you and increase your
numbers. He will bless the fruit of your womb,
the crops of your land—your grain, new wine
and olive oil—the calves of your herds and the
lambs of your flocks in the land he swore to your
ancestors to give you. (Deuteronomy 7:13)

The fruit of your womb will be blessed, and
the crops of your land and the young of your
livestock—the calves of your herds and the
lambs of your flocks. (Deuteronomy 28:4)

Then the Lord your God will make you most
prosperous in all the work of your hands and in the
fruit of your womb, the young of your livestock
and the crops of your land. The Lord will again
delight in you and make you prosperous, just as he
delighted in your ancestors. (Deuteronomy 30:9)

The righteous will flourish like a palm tree, they
will grow like a cedar of Lebanon; planted in the

house of the Lord, they will flourish in the courts
of our God. They will still bear fruit in old age, they
will stay fresh and green (Psalm 92:12-14)

The Lord made his people very fruitful; he made
them too numerous for their foes. (Psalm 105:24)

They sowed fields and planted vineyards that
yielded a fruitful harvest; he blessed them, and
their numbers greatly increased, and he did not
let their herds diminish. (Psalm 107:37-38)

"Don't you have a saying, 'It's still four months until
harvest'? I tell you, open your eyes and look at the
fields! They are ripe for harvest. Even now the one who
reaps draws a wage and harvests a crop for eternal
life, so that the sower and the reaper may be glad
together. Thus the saying 'One sows and another reaps'
is true. I sent you to reap what you have not worked
for. Others have done the hard work, and you have
reaped the benefits of their labor." (John 4:35-38)

"I am the true vine, and my Father is the gardener. He
cuts off every branch in me that bears no fruit, while
every branch that does bear fruit he prunes so that it will
be even more fruitful. You are already clean because of
the word I have spoken to you. Remain in me, as I also
remain in you. No branch can bear fruit by itself; it must
remain in the vine. Neither can you bear fruit unless you
remain in me. "I am the vine; you are the branches. If you
remain in me and I in you, you will bear much fruit; apart
from me you can do nothing. If you do not remain in me,
you are like a branch that is thrown away and withers;
such branches are picked up, thrown into the fire and
burned. If you remain in me and my words remain in
you, ask whatever you wish, and it will be done for you.
This is to my Father's glory, that you bear much fruit,

showing yourselves to be my disciples. (John 15:1-8)

You did not choose me, but I chose you and appointed
you so that you might go and bear fruit—fruit
that will last—and so that whatever you ask in my
name the Father will give you. (John 15:16)

GOD'S FAITHFULNESS

And he passed in front of Moses, proclaiming, "The Lord, the Lord, the compassionate and gracious God, slow to anger, abounding in love and faithfulness, maintaining love to thousands, and forgiving wickedness, rebellion and sin. Yet he does not leave the guilty unpunished; he punishes the children and their children for the sin of the parents to the third and fourth generation." (Exodus 34:6–7)

Your love, Lord, reaches to the heavens, your faithfulness to the skies. (Psalm 36:5)

"For a brief moment I abandoned you, but with deep compassion I will bring you back. In a surge of anger I hid my face from you for a moment, but with everlasting kindness I will have compassion on you," says the Lord your Redeemer. "To me this is like the days of Noah, when I swore that the waters of Noah would never again cover the earth. So now I have sworn not to be angry with you, never to rebuke you again. Though the mountains be shaken and the hills be removed, yet my unfailing love for you will not be shaken nor my covenant of peace be removed," says the Lord, who has compassion on you. (Isaiah 54:7-10)

Because of the Lord's great love we are not consumed, for his compassions never fail.

They are new every morning; great is your
faithfulness. (Lamentations 3:22-23)

What advantage, then, is there in being a Jew, or what
value is there in circumcision? Much in every way!
First of all, the Jews have been entrusted with the very
words of God. What if some were unfaithful? Will their
unfaithfulness nullify God's faithfulness? Not at all!
Let God be true, and every human being a liar. As it is
written: "So that you may be proved right when you
speak and prevail when you judge." (Romans 3:1–4)

God is faithful, who has called you into fellowship with
his Son, Jesus Christ our Lord. (1 Corinthians 1:9)

No temptation has overtaken you except what is
common to mankind. And God is faithful; he will not
let you be tempted beyond what you can bear. But
when you are tempted, he will also provide a way out
so that you can endure it. (1 Corinthians 10:13)

May God himself, the God of peace, sanctify you
through and through. May your whole spirit, soul
and body be kept blameless at the coming of our
Lord Jesus Christ. The one who calls you is faithful,
and he will do it. (1 Thessalonians 5:23-24)

But the Lord is faithful, and he will strengthen you and
protect you from the evil one. (2 Thessalonians 3:3)

Here is a trustworthy saying: If we died with him,
we will also live with him; if we endure, we will
also reign with him. If we disown him, he will also
disown us; if we are faithless, he remains faithful, for
he cannot disown himself. (2 Timothy 2:11-13)

Let us hold unswervingly to the hope we profess,
for he who promised is faithful. (Hebrews 10:23)

Jesus Christ is the same yesterday and
today and forever. (Hebrews 13:8)

So then, those who suffer according to God's
will should commit themselves to their faithful
Creator and continue to do good. (1 Peter 4:19)

If we confess our sins, he is faithful and just
and will forgive us our sins and purify us
from all unrighteousness. (1 John 1:9)

GOD'S PROVISION

So Abraham called that place The Lord Will Provide. And to this day it is said, "On the mountain of the Lord it will be provided." (Genesis 22:14)

The Lord is my shepherd, I lack nothing. He makes me lie down in green pastures, he leads me beside quiet waters, (Psalm 23:1-2)

Fear the Lord, you his holy people, for those who fear Him lack nothing. The lions may grow weak and hungry, but those who seek the Lord lack no good thing. (Psalm 34:9-10)

I was young and now I am old, yet I have never seen the righteous forsaken or their children begging bread. (Psalm 37:25)

For the Lord God is a sun and shield; the Lord bestows favor and honor; no good thing does he withhold from those whose walk is blameless. (Psalm 84:11)

"Therefore I tell you, do not worry about your life, what you will eat or drink; or about your body, what you will wear. Is not life more than food, and the body more than clothes? Look at the birds of the air; they do not sow or reap or store away in barns, and yet your heavenly Father feeds them. Are you not much more valuable than they? Can any one of you by worrying add a single hour to your life? "And why do you worry about clothes? See how the flowers of the field grow. They do not labor or spin. Yet I tell you that not even Solomon in all his splendor was dressed like one of these. If that is how God clothes the grass of the field, which is here today and tomorrow is thrown into the fire, will he not much more clothe you—you of little faith? So do not worry, saying, 'What shall we eat?' or 'What shall we drink?' or 'What shall we wear?' For the pagans run after all these things, and your heavenly Father knows that you need them. But seek first his kingdom and his righteousness, and all these things will be given to you as well. Therefore do not worry about tomorrow, for tomorrow will worry about itself. Each day has enough trouble of its own. (Matthew 6:25-34)

Are not five sparrows sold for two pennies? Yet not one of them is forgotten by God. Indeed, the very hairs of your head are all numbered. Don't be afraid; you are worth more than many sparrows. (Luke 12:6-7)

The thief comes only to steal and kill and destroy; I have come that they may have life, and have it to the full. (John 10:10)

He who did not spare his own Son, but gave him up for us all—how will he not also, along with him, graciously give us all things? (Romans 8:32)

And God is able to bless you abundantly, so that in all things at all times, having all that you need, you will abound in every good work. (2 Corinthians 9:8)

Do not be anxious about anything, but in every situation, by prayer and petition, with thanksgiving, present your requests to God. (Philippians 4:6)

And my God will meet all your needs according to the riches of his glory in Christ Jesus. (Philippians 4:19)

Keep your lives free from the love of money
and be content with what you have, because
God has said, "Never will I leave you; never
will I forsake you." (Hebrews 13:5)

His divine power has given us everything we need for
a godly life through our knowledge of him who called
us by his own glory and goodness. (2 Peter 1:3)

GUIDANCE

He guides the humble in what is right and
teaches them his way. All the ways of the Lord are
loving and faithful toward those who keep the
demands of his covenant. (Psalm 25:9-10)

I will instruct you and teach you in the way
you should go; I will counsel you with my
loving eye on you. (Psalm 32:8)

Commit your way to the Lord; trust in him and
he will do this: He will make your righteous
reward shine like the dawn, your vindication
like the noonday sun. (Psalm 37:5-6)

The Lord makes firm the steps of the one who delights
in him; though he may stumble, he will not fall, for the
Lord upholds him with his hand. (Psalm 37:23-24)

You guide me with your counsel, and afterward
you will take me into glory. (Psalm 73:24)

Your word is a lamp for my feet, a light
on my path. (Psalm 119:105)

Trust in the Lord with all your heart and lean not on your
own understanding; in all your ways submit to him,
and he will make your paths straight. (Proverbs 3:5-6)

Whether you turn to the right or to the left,
your ears will hear a voice behind you, saying,

"This is the way; walk in it." (Isaiah 30:21)

The Lord will guide you always; he will satisfy your needs in a sun-scorched land and will strengthen your frame. You will be like a well-watered garden, like a spring whose waters never fail. (Isaiah 58:11)

But seek first his kingdom and his righteousness, and all these things will be given to you as well. (Matthew 6:33)

Immediately the boy's father exclaimed, "I do believe; help me overcome my unbelief!" (Mark 9:24)

But when he, the Spirit of truth, comes, he will guide you into all the truth. He will not speak on his own; he will speak only what he hears, and he will tell you what is yet to come. (John 16:13)

If any of you lacks wisdom, you should ask God, who gives generously to all without finding fault, and it will be given to you. (James 1:5)

GUILT

Then I acknowledged my sin to you and did not cover up my iniquity. I said, "I will confess my transgressions to the Lord." And you forgave the guilt of my sin. (Psalm 32:5)

"Come now, let us settle the matter," says the Lord. "Though your sins are like scarlet, they shall be as white as snow; though they are red as crimson, they shall be like wool. (Isaiah 1:18)

With it he touched my mouth and said, "See, this has touched your lips; your guilt is taken away and your sin atoned for." (Isaiah 6:7)

"I have swept away your offenses like a cloud, your sins like the morning mist. Return to me, for I have redeemed you." (Isaiah 44:22)

Therefore, there is now no condemnation for those who are in Christ Jesus. (Romans 8:1)

What, then, shall we say in response to these things? If God is for us, who can be against us? He who did not spare his own Son, but gave him up for us all—how will he not also, along with him, graciously give us all things? Who will bring any charge against those whom God has chosen? It is God who justifies. Who then is the one who condemns? No one. Christ Jesus who died

—more than that, who was raised to life—is at the right hand of God and is also interceding for us. Who shall separate us from the love of Christ? Shall trouble or hardship or persecution or famine or nakedness or danger or sword? As it is written: "For your sake we face death all day long; we are considered as sheep to be slaughtered." No, in all these things we are more than conquerors through him who loved us. For I am convinced that neither death nor life, neither angels nor demons, neither the present nor the future, nor any powers, neither height nor depth, nor anything else in all creation, will be able to separate us from the love of God that is in Christ Jesus our Lord. (Romans 8:31-39)

Therefore, if anyone is in Christ, the new creation has come: The old has gone, the new is here! (2 Corinthians 5:17)

"For I will forgive their wickedness and will remember their sins no more." (Hebrews 8:12)

Let us draw near to God with a sincere heart and with the full assurance that faith brings, having our hearts sprinkled to cleanse us from a guilty conscience and having our bodies washed with pure water. (Hebrews 10:22)

If we confess our sins, he is faithful and just and will forgive us our sins and purify us from all unrighteousness. (1 John 1:9)

HEALING FOR THOSE WHO ARE FALTERING

Blessed is the one whose transgressions are forgiven, whose sins are covered. Blessed is the one whose sin the Lord does not count against them and in whose spirit is no deceit. When I kept silent, my bones wasted away through my groaning all day long. For day and night your hand was heavy on me; my strength was sapped as in the heat of summer. Then I acknowledged my sin to you and did not cover up my iniquity. I said, "I will confess my transgressions to the Lord." And you forgave the guilt of my sin. (Psalm 32:1-5)

My sacrifice, O God, is a broken spirit; a broken and contrite heart you, God, will not despise. (Psalm 51:17)

For this is what the high and exalted One says—he who lives forever, whose name is holy: "I live in a high and holy place, but also with the one who is contrite and lowly in spirit, to revive the spirit of the lowly and to revive the heart of the contrite. I will not accuse them forever, nor will I always be angry, for then they would faint away because of me—the very people I have created. I was enraged by their sinful greed; I punished them, and hid my face in anger, yet they kept on in their willful ways. I have seen their ways, but I will heal them; I will guide them and restore comfort to Israel's mourners (Isaiah 57:15-18)

Has not my hand made all these things, and so they came into being?" declares the Lord. "These are the ones I look on with favor: those who are humble and contrite in spirit, and who tremble at my word. (Isaiah 66:2)

"Return, faithless people; I will cure you of backsliding."

"Yes, we will come to you, for you are the
Lord our God." (Jeremiah 3:22)

"Come, let us return to the Lord. He has torn us
to pieces but he will heal us; he has injured us
but he will bind up our wounds. (Hosea 6:1)

Take words with you and return to the Lord. Say to
him: "Forgive all our sins and receive us graciously,
that we may offer the fruit of our lips. (Hosea 14:2)

"I will heal their waywardness and love them freely,
for my anger has turned away from them. I will be
like the dew to Israel; he will blossom like a lily. Like
a cedar of Lebanon he will send down his roots; his
young shoots will grow. His splendor will be like an
olive tree, his fragrance like a cedar of Lebanon. People
will dwell again in his shade; they will flourish like the
grain, they will blossom like the vine—Israel's fame
will be like the wine of Lebanon." (Hosea 14:4-7)

Rend your heart and not your garments. Return
to the Lord your God, for he is gracious and
compassionate, slow to anger and abounding in love,
and he relents from sending calamity. (Joel 2:13)

Therefore tell the people: This is what the
Lord Almighty says: 'Return to me,' declares
the Lord Almighty, 'and I will return to you,'
says the Lord Almighty. (Zechariah 1:3)

"I have not come to call the righteous, but sinners to repentance." (Luke 5:32)

I tell you that in the same way there will be more rejoicing in heaven over one sinner who repents than over ninety-nine righteous persons who do not need to repent. (Luke 15:7)

Repent, then, and turn to God, so that your sins may be wiped out, that times of refreshing may come from the Lord. (Acts 3:19)

If we confess our sins, he is faithful and just and will forgive us our sins and purify us from all unrighteousness. (1 John 1:9)

HOPE

Why, my soul, are you downcast? Why so disturbed within me? Put your hope in God, for I will yet praise him, my Savior and my God. (Psalm 42:11)

But those who hope in the Lord will renew their strength. They will soar on wings like eagles; they will run and not grow weary, they will walk and not be faint. (Isaiah 40:31)

For I know the plans I have for you," declares the Lord, "plans to prosper you and not to harm you, plans to give you hope and a future. (Jeremiah 29:11)

And hope does not put us to shame, because God's love has been poured out into our hearts through the Holy Spirit, who has been given to us. (Romans 5:5)

For in this hope we were saved. But hope that is seen is no hope at all. Who hopes for what they already have? But if we hope for what we do not yet have, we wait for it patiently. (Romans 8:24-25)

Be joyful in hope, patient in affliction, faithful in prayer. (Romans 12:12)

May the God of hope fill you with all joy and peace as you trust in him, so that you may overflow with hope by the power of the Holy Spirit. (Romans 15:13)

For our light and momentary troubles are
achieving for us an eternal glory that far
outweighs them all. So we fix our eyes not
on what is seen, but on what is unseen, since
what is seen is temporary, but what is unseen
is eternal. (2 Corinthians 4:17-18)

I pray that the eyes of your heart may be
enlightened in order that you may know
the hope to which he has called you, the
riches of his glorious inheritance in his
holy people. (Ephesians 1:18)

Paul, an apostle of Christ Jesus by the command of God
our Savior and of Christ Jesus our hope. (1 Timothy 1:1)

For the grace of God has appeared that offers salvation
to all people. It teaches us to say "No" to ungodliness and
worldly passions, and to live self-controlled, upright
and godly lives in this present age, while we wait for
the blessed hope—the appearing of the glory of our
great God and Savior, Jesus Christ. (Titus 2:11-13)

Let us hold unswervingly to the hope we profess,
for he who promised is faithful. (Hebrews 10:23)

Praise be to the God and Father of our Lord Jesus
Christ! In his great mercy he has given us new birth
into a living hope through the resurrection of Jesus
Christ from the dead, and into an inheritance that can
never perish, spoil or fade. This inheritance is kept in
heaven for you, who through faith are shielded by God's
power until the coming of the salvation that is ready
to be revealed in the last time. In all this you greatly
rejoice, though now for a little while you may have
had to suffer grief in all kinds of trials. (1 Peter 1:3-6)

And the God of all grace, who called you to his eternal glory in Christ, after you have suffered a little while, will himself restore you and make you strong, firm and steadfast. (1 Peter 5:10)

JOY

Nehemiah said, "Go and enjoy choice food
and sweet drinks, and send some to those
who have nothing prepared. This day is holy
to our Lord. Do not grieve, for the joy of the
Lord is your strength." (Nehemiah 8:10)

You make known to me the path of life; you will
fill me with joy in your presence, with eternal
pleasures at your right hand. (Psalm 16:11)

For his anger lasts only a moment, but his favor
lasts a lifetime; weeping may stay for the night, but
rejoicing comes in the morning. (Psalm 30:5)

You turned my wailing into dancing; you removed
my sackcloth and clothed me with joy. (Psalm 30:11)

Those who sow with tears will reap
with songs of joy. (Psalm 126:5)

But the angel said to them, "Do not be afraid.
I bring you good news that will cause great
joy for all the people." (Luke 2:10)

The thief comes only to steal and kill and
destroy; I have come that they may have life,
and have it to the full. (John 10:10)

I have told you this so that my joy may be in you

and that your joy may be complete. (John 15:11)

Very truly I tell you, you will weep and mourn while the world rejoices. You will grieve, but your grief will turn to joy. A woman giving birth to a child has pain because her time has come; but when her baby is born she forgets the anguish because of her joy that a child is born into the world. So with you: Now is your time of grief, but I will see you again and you will rejoice, and no one will take away your joy. In that day you will no longer ask me anything. Very truly I tell you, my Father will give you whatever you ask in my name. Until now you have not asked for anything in my name. Ask and you will receive, and your joy will be complete. (John 16:20-24)

"I am coming to you now, but I say these things while I am still in the world, so that they may have the full measure of my joy within them." (John 17:13)

May the God of hope fill you with all joy and peace as you trust in him, so that you may overflow with hope by the power of the Holy Spirit. (Romans 15:13)

LONELINESS

Be strong and courageous. Do not be afraid or terrified because of them, for the Lord your God goes with you; he will never leave you nor forsake you. (Deuteronomy 31:6)

Though my father and mother forsake me, the Lord will receive me. (Psalm 27:10)

God is our refuge and strength, an ever-present help in trouble. (Psalm 46:1)

So do not fear, for I am with you; do not be dismayed, for I am your God. I will strengthen you and help you; I will uphold you with my righteous right hand. (Isaiah 41:10)

For I am the Lord your God who takes hold of your right hand and says to you, Do not fear; I will help you. (Isaiah 41:13)

But now, this is what the Lord says—he who created you, Jacob, he who formed you, Israel: "Do not fear, for I have redeemed you; I have summoned you by name; you are mine. When you pass through the waters, I will be with you; and when you pass through the rivers, they will not sweep over you. when you walk through the fire, you will not be burned; the flames will not set you ablaze. (Isaiah 43:1-2)

But Zion said, "The Lord has forsaken
me, the Lord has forgotten me."

Can a mother forget the baby at her breast and
have no compassion on the child she has borne?
Though she may forget, I will not forget you! See,
I have engraved you on the palms of my hands;
your walls are ever before me. (Isaiah 49:14-16)

Though the mountains be shaken and the hills be
removed, yet my unfailing love for you will not be
shaken nor my covenant of peace be removed," says
the Lord, who has compassion on you. (Isaiah 54:10)

The Lord will guide you always; he will satisfy your
needs in a sun-scorched land and will strengthen
your frame. You will be like a well-watered garden,
like a spring whose waters never fail. (Isaiah 58:11)

"And teaching them to obey everything I have
commanded you. And surely I am with you always,
to the very end of the age." (Matthew 28:20)

And I will ask the Father, and he will give you another
advocate to help you and be with you forever— the
Spirit of truth. The world cannot accept him, because
it neither sees him nor knows him. But you know him,
for he lives with you and will be in you. I will not leave
you as orphans; I will come to you. (John 14:16-18)

For our light and momentary troubles are
achieving for us an eternal glory that far
outweighs them all. (2 Corinthians 4:17)

Keep your lives free from the love of money
and be content with what you have, because
God has said, "Never will I leave you; never

will I forsake you." (Hebrews 13:5)

MARRIAGE

The Lord God said, "It is not good for
the man to be alone. I will make a helper
suitable for him." (Genesis 2:18)

He replied, 'The Lord, before whom I have
walked faithfully, will send his angel with you
and make your journey a success, so that you
can get a wife for my son from my own clan and
from my father's family.' (Genesis 24:40)

Wait for the Lord; be strong and take heart
and wait for the Lord. (Psalm 27:14)

Take delight in the Lord, and he will give you the
desires of your heart. Commit your way to the
Lord; trust in him and he will do this: He will make
your righteous reward shine like the dawn, your
vindication like the noonday sun. (Psalm 37:4-6)

For the Lord God is a sun and shield; the Lord bestows
favor and honor; no good thing does he withhold
from those whose walk is blameless. (Psalm 84:11)

He who finds a wife finds what is good and
receives favor from the Lord. (Proverbs 18:22)

But seek first his kingdom and his righteousness, and all
these things will be given to you as well. (Matthew 6:33)

"Ask and it will be given to you; seek and you will find; knock and the door will be opened to you. For everyone who asks receives; the one who seeks finds; and to the one who knocks, the door will be opened. Which of you, if your son asks for bread, will give him a stone? Or if he asks for a fish, will give him a snake? If you, then, though you are evil, know how to give good gifts to your children, how much more will your Father in heaven give good gifts to those who ask him!" (Matthew 7:7-11)

He who did not spare his own Son, but gave him up for us all—how will he not also, along with him, graciously give us all things? (Romans 8:32)

Marriage should be honored by all, and the marriage bed kept pure, for God will judge the adulterer and all the sexually immoral. (Hebrews 13:4)

PEACE

In peace I will lie down and sleep, for you alone, Lord, make me dwell in safety. (Psalm 4:8)

The Lord gives strength to his people; the Lord blesses his people with peace. (Psalm 29:11)

When the Lord takes pleasure in anyone's way, he causes their enemies to make peace with them. (Proverbs 16:7)

You will keep in perfect peace those whose minds are steadfast, because they trust in you. (Isaiah 26:3)

"Though the mountains be shaken and the hills be removed, yet my unfailing love for you will not be shaken nor my covenant of peace be removed," says the Lord, who has compassion on you. (Isaiah 54:10)

Blessed are the peacemakers, for they will be called children of God. (Matthew 5:9)

Peace I leave with you; my peace I give you. I do not give to you as the world gives. Do not let your hearts be troubled and do not be afraid. (John 14:27)

"I have told you these things, so that in me you may have peace. In this world you will have trouble. But take heart! I have overcome the world." (John 16:33)

Therefore, since we have been justified through
faith, we have peace with God through our
Lord Jesus Christ. (Romans 5:1)

May the God of hope fill you with all joy and peace as
you trust in him, so that you may overflow with hope
by the power of the Holy Spirit. (Romans 15:13)

Finally, brothers and sisters, rejoice! Strive for
full restoration, encourage one another, be of
one mind, live in peace. And the God of love and
peace will be with you. (2 Corinthians 13:11)

Do not be anxious about anything, but in every
situation, by prayer and petition, with thanksgiving,
present your requests to God. And the peace of God,
which transcends all understanding, will guard your
hearts and your minds in Christ Jesus. (Philippians 4:6-7)

Now may the Lord of peace himself give you
peace at all times and in every way. The Lord be
with all of you. (2 Thessalonians 3:16)

PERSEVERANCE

But as for you, be strong and do not give up, for
your work will be rewarded. (2 Chronicles 15:7)

"I know that you can do all things; no purpose
of yours can be thwarted. (Job 42:2)

Wait for the Lord; be strong and take heart
and wait for the Lord. (Psalm 27:14)

The Lord makes firm the steps of the one who delights
in him; though he may stumble, he will not fall, for the
Lord upholds him with his hand. (Psalm 37:23-24)

Let your eyes look straight ahead; fix your gaze directly
before you. Give careful thought to the paths for your
feet and be steadfast in all your ways. (Proverbs 4:25-26)

For though the righteous fall seven times,
they rise again, but the wicked stumble when
calamity strikes. (Proverbs 24:16)

Then Jesus said to them, "Suppose you have a friend,
and you go to him at midnight and say, 'Friend, lend
me three loaves of bread; a friend of mine on a journey
has come to me, and I have no food to offer him.' And
suppose the one inside answers, 'Don't bother me. The
door is already locked, and my children and I are in bed.
I can't get up and give you anything.' I tell you, even
though he will not get up and give you the bread because
of friendship, yet because of your shameless audacity he

will surely get up and give you as much as you need."

So I say to you: Ask and it will be given to you;
seek and you will find; knock and the door will be
opened to you. For everyone who asks receives; the
one who seeks finds; and to the one who knocks,
the door will be opened. (Luke 11:5-10)

Then Jesus told his disciples a parable to show them
that they should always pray and not give up. He said:
"In a certain town there was a judge who neither feared
God nor cared what people thought. And there was
a widow in that town who kept coming to him with
the plea, 'Grant me justice against my adversary.'

"For some time he refused. But finally he said to
himself, 'Even though I don't fear God or care
what people think, yet because this widow keeps
bothering me, I will see that she gets justice, so that
she won't eventually come and attack me!'"

And the Lord said, "Listen to what the unjust judge says.
And will not God bring about justice for his chosen
ones, who cry out to him day and night? Will he keep
putting them off? I tell you, he will see that they get
justice, and quickly. However, when the Son of Man
comes, will he find faith on the earth?" (Luke 18:1-8)

Be joyful in hope, patient in affliction,
faithful in prayer. (Romans 12:12)

Do you not know that in a race all the runners
run, but only one gets the prize? Run in such a way
as to get the prize. Everyone who competes in the
games goes into strict training. They do it to get a
crown that will not last, but we do it to get a crown
that will last forever. (1 Corinthians 9:24-25)

Let us not become weary in doing good, for
at the proper time we will reap a harvest if
we do not give up. (Galatians 6:9)

And pray in the Spirit on all occasions with
all kinds of prayers and requests. With this in
mind, be alert and always keep on praying for
all the Lord's people. (Ephesians 6:18)

Being confident of this, that he who began a good
work in you will carry it on to completion until
the day of Christ Jesus. (Philippians 1:6)

Brothers and sisters, I do not consider myself
yet to have taken hold of it. But one thing I do:
Forgetting what is behind and straining toward
what is ahead, I press on toward the goal to win
the prize for which God has called me heavenward
in Christ Jesus. (Philippians 3:13-14)

I have fought the good fight, I have finished the
race, I have kept the faith. Now there is in store for
me the crown of righteousness, which the Lord,
the righteous Judge, will award to me on that day
—and not only to me, but also to all who have
longed for his appearing. (2 Timothy 4:7-8)

So do not throw away your confidence; it will
be richly rewarded. You need to persevere so
that when you have done the will of God, you
will receive what he has promised. For,

"In just a little while,
he who is coming will come
and will not delay."

And, "But my righteous one will live by faith.
And I take no pleasure in the one who shrinks

back." But we do not belong to those who shrink back and are destroyed, but to those who have faith and are saved. (Hebrews 10:35-39)

Therefore, since we are surrounded by such a great cloud of witnesses, let us throw off everything that hinders and the sin that so easily entangles. And let us run with perseverance the race marked out for us, fixing our eyes on Jesus, the pioneer and perfecter of faith. For the joy set before him he endured the cross, scorning its shame, and sat down at the right hand of the throne of God. (Hebrews 12:1-2)

Blessed is the one who perseveres under trial because, having stood the test, that person will receive the crown of life that the Lord has promised to those who love him. (James 1:12)

Is anyone among you in trouble? Let them pray. Is anyone happy? Let them sing songs of praise. Is anyone among you sick? Let them call the elders of the church to pray over them and anoint them with oil in the name of the Lord. And the prayer offered in faith will make the sick person well; the Lord will raise them up. If they have sinned, they will be forgiven. Therefore confess your sins to each other and pray for each other so that you may be healed. The prayer of a righteous person is powerful and effective. Elijah was a human being, even as we are. He prayed earnestly that it would not rain, and it did not rain on the land for three and a half years. Again he prayed, and the heavens gave rain, and the earth produced its crops. (James 5:13-18)

Who through faith are shielded by God's power until the coming of the salvation that is ready to be revealed in the last time. (1 Peter 1:5)

Concerning this salvation, the prophets, who spoke of

the grace that was to come to you, searched intently and with the greatest care, trying to find out the time and circumstances to which the Spirit of Christ in them was pointing when he predicted the sufferings of the Messiah and the glories that would follow. (1 Peter 5:10-11)

To him who is able to keep you from stumbling and to present you before his glorious presence without fault and with great joy— to the only God our Savior be glory, majesty, power and authority, through Jesus Christ our Lord, before all ages, now and forevermore! Amen. (Jude 1:24-25)

PROVIDENCE

You intended to harm me, but God intended it
for good to accomplish what is now being done,
the saving of many lives. (Genesis 50:20)

"Can you fathom the mysteries of God? Can you
probe the limits of the Almighty? They are higher
than the heavens above—what can you do?
They are deeper than the depths below—what
can you know? Their measure is longer than the
earth and wider than the sea. (Job 11:7-9)

The Lord is righteous in all his ways and
faithful in all he does. (Psalm 145:17)

"Therefore I tell you, do not worry about your life,
what you will eat or drink; or about your body, what
you will wear. Is not life more than food, and the
body more than clothes? Look at the birds of the
air; they do not sow or reap or store away in barns,
and yet your heavenly Father feeds them. Are you
not much more valuable than they? Can any one of
you by worrying add a single hour to your life?

"And why do you worry about clothes? See how
the flowers of the field grow. They do not labor or
spin. Yet I tell you that not even Solomon in all his
splendor was dressed like one of these. If that is

how God clothes the grass of the field, which is here today and tomorrow is thrown into the fire, will he not much more clothe you—you of little faith? So do not worry, saying, 'What shall we eat?' or 'What shall we drink?' or 'What shall we wear?' For the pagans run after all these things, and your heavenly Father knows that you need them. But seek first his kingdom and his righteousness, and all these things will be given to you as well. (Matthew 6:25-33)

Are not two sparrows sold for a penny? Yet not one of them will fall to the ground outside your Father's care. And even the very hairs of your head are all numbered. So don't be afraid; you are worth more than many sparrows. (Matthew 10:29-31)

And we know that in all things God works for the good of those who love him, who have been called according to his purpose. (Romans 8:28)

For from him and through him and for him are all things.To him be the glory forever! Amen. (Romans 11:36)

RECONCILIATION

Repent, then, and turn to God, so that your
sins may be wiped out, that times of refreshing
may come from the Lord. (Acts 3:19)

Therefore, since we have been justified through
faith, we have peace with God through our Lord Jesus
Christ, through whom we have gained access by faith
into this grace in which we now stand. And we boast
in the hope of the glory of God. (Romans 5:1-2)

For if, while we were God's enemies, we were reconciled
to him through the death of his Son, how much more,
having been reconciled, shall we be saved through
his life! Not only is this so, but we also boast in God
through our Lord Jesus Christ, through whom we
have now received reconciliation. (Romans 5:10-11)

All this is from God, who reconciled us to himself
through Christ and gave us the ministry of
reconciliation: that God was reconciling the world
to himself in Christ, not counting people's sins
against them. And he has committed to us the
message of reconciliation. We are therefore Christ's
ambassadors, as though God were making his appeal
through us. We implore you on Christ's behalf:
Be reconciled to God. (2 Corinthians 5:18-20)

In him we have redemption through his blood, the forgiveness of sins, in accordance with the riches of God's grace that he lavished on us. With all wisdom and understanding, he made known to us the mystery of his will according to his good pleasure, which he purposed in Christ, to be put into effect when the times reach their fulfillment—to bring unity to all things in heaven and on earth under Christ. (Ephesians 1:7-10)

But now in Christ Jesus you who once were far away have been brought near by the blood of Christ. For he himself is our peace, who has made the two groups one and has destroyed the barrier, the dividing wall of hostility, by setting aside in his flesh the law with its commands and regulations. His purpose was to create in himself one new humanity out of the two, thus making peace, and in one body to reconcile both of them to God through the cross, by which he put to death their hostility. He came and preached peace to you who were far away and peace to those who were near. (Ephesians 2:13-17)

For God was pleased to have all his fullness dwell in him, and through him to reconcile to himself all things, whether things on earth or things in heaven, by making peace through his blood, shed on the cross. Once you were alienated from God and were enemies in your minds because of your evil behavior. But now he has reconciled you by Christ's physical body through death to present you holy in his sight, without blemish and free from accusation. (Colossians 1:19-22)

Bear with each other and forgive one another if any of you has a grievance against someone. Forgive as the Lord forgave you. (Colossians 3:13)

For there is one God and one mediator between God and mankind, the man Christ Jesus. (1 Timothy 2:5)

My dear children, I write this to you so that you will not sin. But if anybody does sin, we have an advocate with the Father—Jesus Christ, the Righteous One. He is the atoning sacrifice for our sins, and not only for ours but also for the sins of the whole world. (1 John 2:1-2)

Renewal

If my people, who are called by my name, will humble themselves and pray and seek my face and turn from their wicked ways, then I will hear from heaven, and I will forgive their sin and will heal their land. Now my eyes will be open and my ears attentive to the prayers offered in this place. (2 Chronicles 7:14-15)

Will you not revive us again, that your people may rejoice in you? (Psalm 85:6)

"The poor and needy search for water, but there is none; their tongues are parched with thirst. But I the Lord will answer them; I, the God of Israel, will not forsake them. I will make rivers flow on barren heights, and springs within the valleys. I will turn the desert into pools of water, and the parched ground into springs." (Isaiah 41:17-18)

For I will pour water on the thirsty land, and streams on the dry ground; I will pour out my Spirit on your offspring, and my blessing on your descendants. They will spring up like grass in a meadow, like poplar trees by flowing streams. Some will say, 'I belong to the Lord'; others will call themselves by the name of Jacob; still others will write on their hand, 'The Lord's,' and will take the name Israel. (Isaiah 44:3-5)

I will make them and the places surrounding my hill a blessing. I will send down showers in season; there will be showers of blessing. (Ezekiel 34:26)

SALVATION

When the disciples heard this, they were greatly
astonished and asked, "Who then can be saved?"

Jesus looked at them and said, "With man
this is impossible, but with God all things
are possible." (Matthew 19:25-26)

For God so loved the world that he gave his one and
only Son, that whoever believes in him shall not
perish but have eternal life. For God did not send
his Son into the world to condemn the world, but
to save the world through him. (John 3:16-17)

Very truly I tell you, the one who believes
has eternal life. (John 6:47)

Jesus answered, "I am the way and the truth
and the life. No one comes to the Father
except through me. (John 14:6)

Peter replied, "Repent and be baptized, every one of you, in
the name of Jesus Christ for the forgiveness of your sins.
And you will receive the gift of the Holy Spirit." (Acts 2:38)

"Salvation is found in no one else, for there is
no other name under heaven given to mankind
by which we must be saved." (Acts 4:12)

"Therefore, my friends, I want you to know that
through Jesus the forgiveness of sins is proclaimed to

you. Through him everyone who believes is set free
from every sin, a justification you were not able to
obtain under the law of Moses." (Acts 13:38-39)

He then brought them out and asked, "Sirs, what must
I do to be saved?" They replied, "Believe in the Lord
Jesus, and you will be saved—you and your household."
Then they spoke the word of the Lord to him and
to all the others in his house. (Acts 16:30-32)

For I am convinced that neither death nor life,
neither angels nor demons, neither the present
nor the future, nor any powers, neither height
nor depth, nor anything else in all creation, will
be able to separate us from the love of God that is
in Christ Jesus our Lord. (Romans 8:38-39)

If you declare with your mouth, "Jesus is Lord," and
believe in your heart that God raised him from the
dead, you will be saved. For it is with your heart that
you believe and are justified, and it is with your mouth
that you profess your faith and are saved. As Scripture
says, "Anyone who believes in him will never be put
to shame." For there is no difference between Jew and
Gentile—the same Lord is Lord of all and richly blesses
all who call on him, for, "Everyone who calls on the
name of the Lord will be saved." (Romans 10:9-13)

For it is by grace you have been saved, through faith—
and this is not from yourselves, it is the gift of God— not
by works, so that no one can boast. (Ephesians 2:8-9)

He saved us, not because of righteous things
we had done, but because of his mercy. He
saved us through the washing of rebirth and
renewal by the Holy Spirit. (Titus 3:5)

Therefore he is able to save completely those who

come to God through him, because he always lives to intercede for them. (Hebrews 7:25)

SEEKING GOD

But if from there you seek the Lord your God, you will find him if you seek him with all your heart and with all your soul. When you are in distress and all these things have happened to you, then in later days you will return to the Lord your God and obey him. For the Lord your God is a merciful God; he will not abandon or destroy you or forget the covenant with your ancestors, which he confirmed to them by oath. (Deuteronomy 4:29-31)

Look to the Lord and his strength; seek his face always. (1 Chronicles 16:11)

"Now devote your heart and soul to seeking the Lord your God. Begin to build the sanctuary of the Lord God, so that you may bring the ark of the covenant of the Lord and the sacred articles belonging to God into the temple that will be built for the Name of the Lord." (1 Chronicles 22:19)

"And you, my son Solomon, acknowledge the God of your father, and serve him with wholehearted devotion and with a willing mind, for the Lord searches every heart and understands every desire and every thought. If you seek him, he will be found by you; but if you forsake him, he will reject you forever." (1 Chronicles 28:9)

If my people, who are called by my name, will humble themselves and pray and seek my face and turn from their wicked ways, then I will

hear from heaven, and I will forgive their sin
and will heal their land. (2 Chronicles 7:14)

Those who know your name trust in you, for you, Lord,
have never forsaken those who seek you. (Psalm 9:10)

But may all who seek you rejoice and be glad in
you; may those who long for your saving help
always say, "The Lord is great!" (Psalm 40:16)

I love those who love me, and those who
seek me find me. (Proverbs 8:17)

I have not spoken in secret, from somewhere
in a land of darkness; I have not said to Jacob's
descendants, 'Seek me in vain.' I, the Lord, speak
the truth; I declare what is right. (Isaiah 45:19)

Then you will call on me and come and pray to me,
and I will listen to you. You will seek me and find me
when you seek me with all your heart. I will be found
by you," declares the Lord, "and will bring you back
from captivity. I will gather you from all the nations
and places where I have banished you," declares the
Lord, "and will bring you back to the place from
which I carried you into exile." (Jeremiah 29:12-14)

The Lord is good to those whose hope is in him,
to the one who seeks him. (Lamentations 3:25)

"I will send my messenger, who will prepare the
way before me. Then suddenly the Lord you are
seeking will come to his temple; the messenger
of the covenant, whom you desire, will come,"
says the Lord Almighty. (Malachi 3:1)

But seek first his kingdom and his righteousness, and all
these things will be given to you as well. (Matthew 6:33)

"The kingdom of heaven is like treasure hidden in a field. When a man found it, he hid it again, and then in his joy went and sold all he had and bought that field. "Again, the kingdom of heaven is like a merchant looking for fine pearls. When he found one of great value, he went away and sold everything he had and bought it. (Matthew 13:44-46)

"So I say to you: Ask and it will be given to you; seek and you will find; knock and the door will be opened to you. For everyone who asks receives; the one who seeks finds; and to the one who knocks, the door will be opened." (Luke 11:9-10)

God did this so that they would seek him and perhaps reach out for him and find him, though he is not far from any one of us. (Acts 17:27)

And without faith it is impossible to please God, because anyone who comes to him must believe that he exists and that he rewards those who earnestly seek him. (Hebrews 11:6)

Come near to God and he will come near to you. Wash your hands, you sinners, and purify your hearts, you double-minded. (James 4:8)

SLEEPLESSNESS

I lie down and sleep; I wake again, because
the Lord sustains me. (Psalm 3:5)

In peace I will lie down and sleep, for you alone,
Lord, make me dwell in safety. (Psalm 4:8)

He says, "Be still, and know that I am God;
I will be exalted among the nations, I will be
exalted in the earth." (Psalm 46:10)

Return to your rest, my soul, for the Lord
has been good to you. (Psalm 116:7)

When you lie down, you will not be afraid; when
you lie down, your sleep will be sweet. Have no fear
of sudden disaster or of the ruin that overtakes the
wicked, for the Lord will be at your side and will keep
your foot from being snared. (Proverbs 3:24-26)

You will keep in perfect peace those whose minds are
steadfast, because they trust in you. (Isaiah 26:3)

"Come to me, all you who are weary and burdened,
and I will give you rest. Take my yoke upon you and
learn from me, for I am gentle and humble in heart,
and you will find rest for your souls. For my yoke is
easy and my burden is light." (Matthew 11:28-30)

Peace I leave with you; my peace I give you. I do not

give to you as the world gives. Do not let your hearts
be troubled and do not be afraid. (John 14:27)

SUFFERING

The righteous person may have many troubles, but the Lord delivers him from them all. (Psalm 34:19)

When you pass through the waters, I will be with you; and when you pass through the rivers, they will not sweep over you. When you walk through the fire, you will not be burned; the flames will not set you ablaze. (Isaiah 43:2)

Blessed are those who are persecuted because of righteousness, for theirs is the kingdom of heaven. "Blessed are you when people insult you, persecute you and falsely say all kinds of evil against you because of me. Rejoice and be glad, because great is your reward in heaven, for in the same way they persecuted the prophets who were before you. (Matthew 5:10-12)

"I have told you these things, so that in me you may have peace. In this world you will have trouble. But take heart! I have overcome the world." (John 16:33)

Not only so, but we also glory in our sufferings, because we know that suffering produces perseverance. (Romans 5:3)

I consider that our present sufferings are not worth comparing with the glory that will be revealed in us. (Romans 8:18)

Who shall separate us from the love of Christ? Shall trouble or hardship or persecution or famine or nakedness or danger or sword? As it is written:

"For your sake we face death all day long;
we are considered as sheep to be slaughtered."

No, in all these things we are more than conquerors through him who loved us. For I am convinced that neither death nor life, neither angels nor demons, neither the present nor the future, nor any powers, neither height nor depth, nor anything else in all creation, will be able to separate us from the love of God that is in Christ Jesus our Lord. (Romans 8:35-39)

Praise be to the God and Father of our Lord Jesus Christ, the Father of compassion and the God of all comfort, who comforts us in all our troubles, so that we can comfort those in any trouble with the comfort we ourselves receive from God. For just as we share abundantly in the sufferings of Christ, so also our comfort abounds through Christ. If we are distressed, it is for your comfort and salvation; if we are comforted, it is for your comfort, which produces in you patient endurance of the same sufferings we suffer. And our hope for you is firm, because we know that just as you share in our sufferings, so also you share in our comfort. (2 Corinthians 1:3-7)

Therefore we do not lose heart. Though outwardly we are wasting away, yet inwardly we are being renewed day by day. For our light and momentary troubles are achieving for us an eternal glory that far outweighs them all. So we fix our eyes not on what is seen, but on what is unseen, since what is seen is temporary, but what is unseen is eternal. (2 Corinthians 4:16-18)

In fact, everyone who wants to live a godly life in
Christ Jesus will be persecuted. (2 Timothy 3:12)

Blessed is the one who perseveres under trial
because, having stood the test, that person
will receive the crown of life that the Lord has
promised to those who love him. (James 1:12)

Brothers and sisters, as an example of patience in the face
of suffering, take the prophets who spoke in the name
of the Lord. As you know, we count as blessed those who
have persevered. You have heard of Job's perseverance
and have seen what the Lord finally brought about. The
Lord is full of compassion and mercy. (James 5:10-11)

Is anyone among you in trouble? Let
them pray. Is anyone happy? Let them
sing songs of praise. (James 5:13)

Who is going to harm you if you are eager to do good?
But even if you should suffer for what is right, you are
blessed. "Do not fear their threats; do not be frightened."
But in your hearts revere Christ as Lord. Always be
prepared to give an answer to everyone who asks you
to give the reason for the hope that you have. But
do this with gentleness and respect, keeping a clear
conscience, so that those who speak maliciously against
your good behavior in Christ may be ashamed of their
slander. For it is better, if it is God's will, to suffer for
doing good than for doing evil. (1 Peter 3:13-17)

For it is commendable if someone bears up under
the pain of unjust suffering because they are
conscious of God. But how is it to your credit if you
receive a beating for doing wrong and endure it?
But if you suffer for doing good and you endure it,
this is commendable before God. To this you were

called, because Christ suffered for you, leaving you
an example, that you should follow in his steps.

"He committed no sin,
and no deceit was found in his mouth."

Dear friends, do not be surprised at the fiery ordeal
that has come on you to test you, as though something
strange were happening to you. But rejoice inasmuch as
you participate in the sufferings of Christ, so that you
may be overjoyed when his glory is revealed. If you are
insulted because of the name of Christ, you are blessed,
for the Spirit of glory and of God rests on you. If you
suffer, it should not be as a murderer or thief or any
other kind of criminal, or even as a meddler. However,
if you suffer as a Christian, do not be ashamed, but
praise God that you bear that name. (1 Peter 4:12-16)

So then, those who suffer according to God's will
should commit themselves to their faithful Creator
and continue to do good. (1 Peter 4:19)

And the God of all grace, who called you to his
eternal glory in Christ, after you have suffered
a little while, will himself restore you and make
you strong, firm and steadfast. (1 Peter 5:10)

He will wipe every tear from their eyes. There will be
no more death' or mourning or crying or pain, for the
old order of things has passed away. (Revelation 21:4)

TEMPTATION

Do not be wise in your own eyes; fear the Lord and shun evil. This will bring health to your body and nourishment to your bones. (Proverbs 3:7-8)

And lead us not into temptation, but deliver us from the evil one. And lead us not into temptation, but deliver us from evil. (Matthew 6:13)

No temptation has overtaken you except what is common to mankind. And God is faithful; he will not let you be tempted beyond what you can bear. But when you are tempted, he will also provide a way out so that you can endure it. (1 Corinthians 10:13)

For surely it is not angels he helps, but Abraham's descendants. For this reason he had to be made like them, fully human in every way, in order that he might become a merciful and faithful high priest in service to God, and that he might make atonement for the sins of the people. Because he himself suffered when he was tempted, he is able to help those who are being tempted. (Hebrews 2:16-18)

Therefore, since we have a great high priest who has ascended into heaven, Jesus the Son of God, let us hold firmly to the faith we profess. For we do not have a high priest who is unable to empathize with our weaknesses, but we have one who has been tempted in every way, just as we are—yet he did not sin. Let us then approach God's throne of grace with confidence, so that we may receive mercy and find grace to help us in our time of need. (Hebrews 4:14-16)

When tempted, no one should say, "God is tempting me." For God cannot be tempted by evil, nor does he tempt anyone; but each person is tempted when they are dragged away by their own evil desire and enticed. Then, after desire has conceived, it gives birth to sin; and sin, when it is full-grown, gives birth to death. (James 1:13-15)

THE HOLY SPIRIT

The Spirit of the Lord will come powerfully upon you, and you will prophesy with them; and you will be changed into a different person. (1 Samuel 10:6)

"So I say to you: Ask and it will be given to you; seek and you will find; knock and the door will be opened to you. For everyone who asks receives; the one who seeks finds; and to the one who knocks, the door will be opened. "Which of you fathers, if your son asks for a fish, will give him a snake instead? Or if he asks for an egg, will give him a scorpion? If you then, though you are evil, know how to give good gifts to your children, how much more will your Father in heaven give the Holy Spirit to those who ask him!" (Luke 11:9-13)

And I will ask the Father, and he will give you another advocate to help you and be with you forever— the Spirit of truth. The world cannot accept him, because it neither sees him nor knows him. But you know him, for he lives with you and will be in you. I will not leave you as orphans; I will come to you. (John 14:16-18)

But the Advocate, the Holy Spirit, whom the Father will send in my name, will teach you all things and will remind you of everything I have said to you. (John 14:26)

But you will receive power when the Holy Spirit

comes on you; and you will be my witnesses
in Jerusalem, and in all Judea and Samaria,
and to the ends of the earth." (Acts 1:8)

TRIALS

You intended to harm me, but God intended it
for good to accomplish what is now being done,
the saving of many lives. (Genesis 50:20)

But he knows the way that I take; when he has
tested me, I will come forth as gold. (Job 23:10)

Trust in the Lord with all your heart and
lean not on your own understanding; in all
your ways submit to him, and he will make
your paths straight. (Proverbs 3:5-6)

But since they have no root, they last only a short
time. When trouble or persecution comes because
of the word, they quickly fall away. (Mark 4:17)

Not only so, but we also glory in our sufferings,
because we know that suffering produces
perseverance; perseverance, character; and
character, hope. (Romans 5:3-4)

I consider that our present sufferings are
not worth comparing with the glory that
will be revealed in us. (Romans 8:18)

Who shall separate us from the love of Christ? Shall
trouble or hardship or persecution or famine or
nakedness or danger or sword? As it is written:

"For your sake we face death all day long;
we are considered as sheep to be slaughtered."

No, in all these things we are more than conquerors through him who loved us. For I am convinced that neither death nor life, neither angels nor demons, neither the present nor the future, nor any powers, neither height nor depth, nor anything else in all creation, will be able to separate us from the love of God that is in Christ Jesus our Lord. (Romans 8:35-39)

No temptation has overtaken you except what is common to mankind. And God is faithful; he will not let you be tempted beyond what you can bear. But when you are tempted, he will also provide a way out so that you can endure it. (1 Corinthians 10:13)

Praise be to the God and Father of our Lord Jesus Christ, the Father of compassion and the God of all comfort, who comforts us in all our troubles, so that we can comfort those in any trouble with the comfort we ourselves receive from God. For just as we share abundantly in the sufferings of Christ, so also our comfort abounds through Christ. (2 Corinthians 1:3-5)

But he said to me, "My grace is sufficient for you, for my power is made perfect in weakness." Therefore I will boast all the more gladly about my weaknesses, so that Christ's power may rest on me. That is why, for Christ's sake, I delight in weaknesses, in insults, in hardships, in persecutions, in difficulties. For when I am weak, then I am strong. (2 Corinthians 12:9-10)

Do not be anxious about anything, but in every situation, by prayer and petition, with thanksgiving, present your requests to God. And the peace of God, which transcends all

understanding, will guard your hearts and your
minds in Christ Jesus. (Philippians 4:6-7)

I can do all this through him who gives
me strength. (Philippians 4:13)

For surely it is not angels he helps, but Abraham's
descendants. For this reason he had to be made like
them, fully human in every way, in order that he
might become a merciful and faithful high priest in
service to God, and that he might make atonement
for the sins of the people. Because he himself
suffered when he was tempted, he is able to help
those who are being tempted. (Hebrews 2:16-18)

Therefore, since we have a great high priest who has
ascended into heaven, Jesus the Son of God, let us
hold firmly to the faith we profess. For we do not have
a high priest who is unable to empathize with our
weaknesses, but we have one who has been tempted
in every way, just as we are—yet he did not sin. Let us
then approach God's throne of grace with confidence,
so that we may receive mercy and find grace to
help us in our time of need. (Hebrews 4:14-16)

Consider it pure joy, my brothers and sisters, whenever
you face trials of many kinds, because you know that
the testing of your faith produces perseverance. Let
perseverance finish its work so that you may be mature
and complete, not lacking anything. (James 1:2-4)

Blessed is the one who perseveres under trial
because, having stood the test, that person
will receive the crown of life that the Lord has
promised to those who love him. (James 1:12)

In all this you greatly rejoice, though now for a
little while you may have had to suffer grief in all

kinds of trials. These have come so that the proven genuineness of your faith—of greater worth than gold, which perishes even though refined by fire —may result in praise, glory and honor when Jesus Christ is revealed. (1 Peter 1:6-7)

So then, those who suffer according to God's will should commit themselves to their faithful Creator and continue to do good. (1 Peter 4:19)

And the God of all grace, who called you to his eternal glory in Christ, after you have suffered a little while, will himself restore you and make you strong, firm and steadfast. To him be the power for ever and ever. Amen. (1 Peter 5:10-11)

TROUBLE

The Lord himself goes before you and will be with you; he will never leave you nor forsake you. Do not be afraid; do not be discouraged. (Deuteronomy 31:8)

The Lord is a refuge for the oppressed, a stronghold in times of trouble. Those who know your name trust in you, for you, Lord, have never forsaken those who seek you. (Psalm 9:9-10)

The Lord is my light and my salvation—whom shall I fear? The Lord is the stronghold of my life —of whom shall I be afraid? (Psalm 27:1)

For in the day of trouble he will keep me safe in his dwelling; he will hide me in the shelter of his sacred tent and set me high upon a rock. (Psalm 27:5)

I will be glad and rejoice in your love,
for you saw my affliction and knew the
anguish of my soul. (Psalm 31:7)

You are my hiding place; you will protect
me from trouble and surround me with
songs of deliverance. (Psalm 32:7)

This poor man called, and the Lord heard him; he saved him out of all his troubles. (Psalm 34:6)

The righteous cry out, and the Lord hears them; he delivers them from all their troubles. (Psalm 34:17)

The salvation of the righteous comes from the Lord; he is their stronghold in time of trouble. (Psalm 37:39)

God is our refuge and strength, an ever-present help in trouble. Therefore we will not fear, though the earth give way and the mountains fall into the heart of the sea, though its waters roar and foam and the mountains quake with their surging. (Psalm 46:1-3)

"Sacrifice thank offerings to God, fulfill your vows to the Most High, and call on me in the day of trouble; I will deliver you, and you will honor me." (Psalm 50: 14-15)

Give us aid against the enemy, for human help is worthless. (Psalm 60:11)

Though you have made me see troubles, many and bitter, you will restore my life again; from the depths of the earth you will again bring me up. (Psalm 71:20)

When I am in distress, I call to you, because you answer me. (Psalm 86:7)

He will call on me, and I will answer him; I will be with him in trouble, I will deliver him and honor him. With long life I will satisfy him and show him my salvation. (Psalm 91:15-16)

Then they cried out to the Lord in their trouble, and he delivered them from their distress. (Psalm 107:6)

Though I walk in the midst of trouble, you preserve my life. You stretch out your hand against the anger of my foes; with your right hand you save me. (Psalm 138:7)

So do not fear, for I am with you; do not be dismayed, for I am your God. I will strengthen you and help you; I will uphold you with my righteous right hand. (Isaiah 41:10)

"For I know the plans I have for you," declares the Lord, "plans to prosper you and not to harm you, plans to give you hope and a future. Then you will call on me and come and pray to me, and I will listen to you. You will seek me and find me when you seek me with all your heart." (Jeremiah 29:11-13)

Because of the Lord's great love we are not consumed, for his compassions never fail. They are new every morning; great is your faithfulness. (Lamentations 3:22-23)

The Lord is good, a refuge in times of trouble. He cares for those who trust in him (Nahum 1:7)

Peace I leave with you; my peace I give you. I do not give to you as the world gives. Do not let your hearts be troubled and do not be afraid. (John 14:27)

"I have told you these things, so that in me you may have peace. In this world you will have trouble. But take heart! I have overcome the world." (John 16:33)

VICTORY OVER SIN

"She will give birth to a son, and you are to give
him the name Jesus, because he will save his
people from their sins." (Matthew 1:21)

Jesus replied, "Very truly I tell you, everyone who sins
is a slave to sin. Now a slave has no permanent place in
the family, but a son belongs to it forever. So if the Son
sets you free, you will be free indeed. (John 8:34-36)

The law was brought in so that the trespass
might increase. But where sin increased, grace
increased all the more. (Romans 5:20)

What shall we say, then? Shall we go on sinning so
that grace may increase? By no means! We are those
who have died to sin; how can we live in it any longer?
Or don't you know that all of us who were baptized
into Christ Jesus were baptized into his death? We
were therefore buried with him through baptism into
death in order that, just as Christ was raised from
the dead through the glory of the Father, we too may
live a new life. For if we have been united with him
in a death like his, we will certainly also be united
with him in a resurrection like his. (Romans 6:1-5)

For sin shall no longer be your master, because you are
not under the law, but under grace. (Romans 6:14)

No temptation has overtaken you except what is

common to mankind. And God is faithful; he will not let you be tempted beyond what you can bear. But when you are tempted, he will also provide a way out so that you can endure it. (1 Corinthians 10:13)

But thanks be to God! He gives us the victory through our Lord Jesus Christ. (1 Corinthians 15:57)

Finally, be strong in the Lord and in his mighty power. Put on the full armor of God, so that you can take your stand against the devil's schemes. For our struggle is not against flesh and blood, but against the rulers, against the authorities, against the powers of this dark world and against the spiritual forces of evil in the heavenly realms. Therefore put on the full armor of God, so that when the day of evil comes, you may be able to stand your ground, and after you have done everything, to stand. (Ephesians 6:10-13)

I can do all this through him who gives me strength. (Philippians 4:13)

ou, dear children, are from God and have overcome them, because the one who is in you is greater than the one who is in the world. (1 John 4:4)

WAITING ON GOD

In you, Lord my God, I put my trust. I trust in you;
do not let me be put to shame, nor let my enemies
triumph over me. No one who hopes in you will ever
be put to shame, but shame will come on those who
are treacherous without cause. (Psalm 25:1-3)

Wait for the Lord; be strong and take heart
and wait for the Lord. (Psalm 27:14)

Be still before the Lord and wait patiently for him;
do not fret when people succeed in their ways, when
they carry out their wicked schemes. Refrain from anger
and turn from wrath; do not fret—it leads only to evil.
For those who are evil will be destroyed, but those who
hope in the Lord will inherit the land. (Psalm 37:7-9)

Hope in the Lord and keep his way. He will exalt
you to inherit the land; when the wicked are
destroyed, you will see it. (Psalm 37:34)

I waited patiently for the Lord; he turned to me and
heard my cry. He lifted me out of the slimy pit, out of
the mud and mire; he set my feet on a rock and gave
me a firm place to stand. He put a new song in my
mouth, a hymn of praise to our God. Many will see and
fear the Lord and put their trust in him. (Psalm 40:1-3)

Yes, my soul, find rest in God; my hope
comes from him. (Psalm 62:5)

Yet the Lord longs to be gracious to you;
therefore he will rise up to show you
compassion. For the Lord is a God of justice.
Blessed are all who wait for him! (Isaiah 30:18)

But those who hope in the Lord will renew
their strength. They will soar on wings like
eagles; they will run and not grow weary, they
will walk and not be faint. (Isaiah 40:31)

Since ancient times no one has heard, no ear has
perceived, no eye has seen any God besides you, who
acts on behalf of those who wait for him. (Isaiah 64:4)

The Lord is good to those whose hope is in him, to
the one who seeks him; it is good to wait quietly for
the salvation of the Lord. (Lamentations 3:25-26)

WEARINESS

When I called, you answered me; you greatly
emboldened me. (Psalm 138:3)

Do you not know? Have you not heard? The Lord is the
everlasting God, the Creator of the ends of the earth.
He will not grow tired or weary, and his understanding
no one can fathom. He gives strength to the weary and
increases the power of the weak. (Isaiah 40:28-29)

But those who hope in the Lord will renew their
strength. They will soar on wings like eagles;
they will run and not grow weary, they will
walk and not be faint. (Isaiah 40:31)

"I will refresh the weary and satisfy
the faint." (Jeremiah 31:25)

The Sovereign Lord is my strength; he makes my
feet like the feet of a deer, he enables me to tread
on the heights. For the director of music. On my
stringed instruments. (Habakkuk 3:19)

"Come to me, all you who are weary and burdened,
and I will give you rest. Take my yoke upon you and
learn from me, for I am gentle and humble in heart,
and you will find rest for your souls. For my yoke is
easy and my burden is light." (Matthew 11:28-30)

Therefore, my dear brothers and sisters, stand firm.
Let nothing move you. Always give yourselves fully
to the work of the Lord, because you know that your
labor in the Lord is not in vain. (1 Corinthians 15:58)

Let us not become weary in doing good, for
at the proper time we will reap a harvest if
we do not give up. (Galatians 6:9)

And as for you, brothers and sisters,
never tire of doing what is good.
(2 Thessalonians 3:13)

Consider him who endured such opposition
from sinners, so that you will not grow
weary and lose heart. (Hebrews 12:3)

WISDOM

The law of the Lord is perfect, refreshing the soul.
The statutes of the Lord are trustworthy, making
wise the simple. The precepts of the Lord are right,
giving joy to the heart. The commands of the Lord
are radiant, giving light to the eyes. The fear of the
Lord is pure, enduring forever. The decrees of the
Lord are firm, and all of them are righteous. They
are more precious than gold, than much pure gold;
they are sweeter than honey, than honey from the
honeycomb. By them your servant is warned; in
keeping them there is great reward. (Psalm 19:7-11)

Oh, how I love your law! I meditate on it all day long.
Your commands are always with me and make me
wiser than my enemies. I have more insight than all
my teachers, for I meditate on your statutes. I have
more understanding than the elders, for I obey your
precepts. I have kept my feet from every evil path so
that I might obey your word. I have not departed from
your laws, for you yourself have taught me. How sweet
are your words to my taste, sweeter than honey to
my mouth! I gain understanding from your precepts;
therefore I hate every wrong path. (Psalm 119:97-104)

My son, if you accept my words and store up my
commands within you, turning your ear to wisdom
and applying your heart to understanding—

indeed, if you call out for insight and cry aloud for understanding, and if you look for it as for silver and search for it as for hidden treasure, then you will understand the fear of the Lord and find the knowledge of God. For the Lord gives wisdom; from his mouth come knowledge and understanding. He holds success in store for the upright. (Proverbs 2:1-7)

The fear of the Lord is the beginning of wisdom, and knowledge of the Holy One is understanding. (Proverbs 9:10)

For I will give you words and wisdom that none of your adversaries will be able to resist or contradict. (Luke 21:15)

It is because of him that you are in Christ Jesus, who has become for us wisdom from God—that is, our righteousness, holiness and redemption. (1 Corinthians 1:30)

I keep asking that the God of our Lord Jesus Christ, the glorious Father, may give you the Spirit of wisdom and revelation, so that you may know him better. (Ephesians 1:17)

My goal is that they may be encouraged in heart and united in love, so that they may have the full riches of complete understanding, in order that they may know the mystery of God, namely, Christ, in whom are hidden all the treasures of wisdom and knowledge. (Colossians 2:2-3)

If any of you lacks wisdom, you should ask God, who gives generously to all without finding fault, and it will be given to you. (James 1:5)

WORRY

Cast your cares on the Lord and he will sustain you; he will never let the righteous be shaken. (Psalm 55:22)

"Therefore I tell you, do not worry about your life, what you will eat or drink; or about your body, what you will wear. Is not life more than food, and the body more than clothes? Look at the birds of the air; they do not sow or reap or store away in barns, and yet your heavenly Father feeds them. Are you not much more valuable than they? Can any one of you by worrying add a single hour to your life?

"And why do you worry about clothes? See how the flowers of the field grow. They do not labor or spin. Yet I tell you that not even Solomon in all his splendor was dressed like one of these. If that is how God clothes the grass of the field, which is here today and tomorrow is thrown into the fire, will he not much more clothe you—you of little faith? So do not worry, saying, 'What shall we eat?' or 'What shall we drink?' or 'What shall we wear?' For the pagans run after all these things, and your heavenly Father knows that you need them. But seek first his kingdom and his righteousness, and all these things will be given to you as well. Therefore do not worry about tomorrow, for tomorrow will worry about itself. Each day has enough trouble of its own. (Matthew 6:25-34)

Then Jesus said to his disciples: "Therefore I tell you, do not worry about your life, what you will eat; or about your body, what you will wear. For life is more than food, and the body more than clothes. Consider the ravens: They do not sow or reap, they have no storeroom or barn; yet God feeds them. And how much more valuable you are than birds! Who of you by worrying can add a single hour to your life? Since you cannot do this very little thing, why do you worry about the rest? (Luke 12:22-26)

Do not be anxious about anything, but in every situation, by prayer and petition, with thanksgiving, present your requests to God. And the peace of God, which transcends all understanding, will guard your hearts and your minds in Christ Jesus. (Philippians 4:6-7)

Cast all your anxiety on him because he cares for you. (1 Peter 5:7)

THE GREATEST LOVE OF ALL

The Vine and the Branches

"I am the true vine, and my Father is the gardener. He cuts off every branch in me that bears no fruit, while every branch that does bear fruit he prunes so that it will be even more fruitful. You are already clean because of the word I have spoken to you. Remain in me, as I also remain in you. No branch can bear fruit by itself; it must remain in the vine. Neither can you bear fruit unless you remain in me.

"I am the vine; you are the branches. If you remain in me and I in you, you will bear much fruit; apart from me you can do nothing. If you do not remain in me, you are like a branch that is thrown away and withers; such branches are picked up, thrown into the fire and burned. If you remain in me and my words remain in you, ask whatever you wish, and it will be done for you. This is to my Father's glory, that you bear much fruit, showing yourselves to be my disciples.

"As the Father has loved me, so have I loved you. Now remain in my love. If you keep my commands, you will remain in my love, just as I have kept my Father's commands and remain in his love. I have told you this so that my joy may be in you and that your joy may be complete. My command is this: Love each other as I have loved you. Greater love has no one than this: to lay down one's life for one's friends. You are my friends if you do what I command. I no longer call you servants, because a servant does not know his master's business. Instead, I have called you friends, for everything that I learned from my Father I have made known to you. You did not choose me, but I chose you and appointed you so that you might go and bear fruit—fruit that will last —and so that whatever you ask in my name the Father will give you. This is my command: Love each other.

The World Hates the Disciples

"If the world hates you, keep in mind that it hated me first. If you belonged to the world, it would love you as its own. As it is, you do not belong to the world, but I have chosen you out of the world. That is why the world hates you. Remember what I told you: 'A servant is not greater than his master.' If they persecuted me, they will persecute you also. If they obeyed my teaching, they will obey yours also. They will treat you this way because of my name, for they do not know the one who sent me. If I had not come and spoken to them, they would not be guilty of sin; but now they have no excuse for their sin. Whoever hates me hates my Father as well. If I had not done among them the works no one else did, they would not be guilty of sin. As it is, they have seen, and yet they have hated both me and my Father. But this is to fulfill what is written in their Law: 'They hated me without reason.'

The Work of the Holy Spirit

"When the Advocate comes, whom I will send to you from the Father—the Spirit of truth who goes out from the Father—he will testify about me. And you also must testify, for you have been with me from the beginning.

ABOUT THE AUTHOR

Chris Cavanagh

Fiction author and self-help wizard, Chris Cavanagh loves to share both his imagination and life experience through writing. Wanting to travel the world, Chris completed his post graduate studies in Canberra, Australia. He has lived in Australia, Germany, Britain, and Canada. Chris would always say that his family is the  most important part of his life, and he enjoys spending as much time with them as possible. Chris has a witty sense of humour, and his writing is sure to make you laugh. He is a parent, coach, teacher, and author, who loves life and everything it has to offer.

BOOKS BY THIS AUTHOR

The Secret To Gratitude: 30 Practical Ways To Deepen The Feelings Of Gratitude In Your Life

Do you want to improve your relationships, your mental health and well-being, and just be happier in your life?

It can be so easy to fall into the trap of feeling dissatisfied with life. We often look at what others have or the places they go and want to have it too, usually making ourselves feel worse because we don't. With social media being as prevalent as it is in today's society, feelings of envy or low self-worth are at an all-time high. It's not good. In fact, we're in the midst of a mental health crisis.

Gratitude is one of the most important things we can do to appreciate what we have in our lives. It allows us to focus on what we have and be grateful for it, regardless of whether we are driving the car of our dreams, have met that special person, or work at the job we dream about. It can also be a very effective tool when using the Law of Attraction to manifest your best life.

In our busy and stressful lives, how do we find the time to practice and deepen the feelings of gratitude? This short, no nonsense book contains 30 of the best and easiest ways to do that! You can try them all, or choose the ones that you think will work the best for you.

The Secret to Gratitude can help you improve you life starting today. This isn't just another blank journal that asks you to figure out how to be more grateful on your own. Each chapter describes fun and engaging ways that take very little time to accomplish. Take gratitude for a test drive and see where it takes you. You will be happy you did!

That Secret Feeling: 30 Practical Ways To Give You The Feeling Needed To Effectively Use The Law Of Attraction

Have you been trying to use the Law of Attraction but haven't had the kind of success you were hoping for? I had the same problem. I just couldn't feel the way I needed to when I tried to visualize the things I wanted to attract into my life. Life is busy and stressful, and it's not always easy to be in a good mood, especially the kind of mood you need to successfully use the Law of Attraction. I was stuck, and I bet you are too.

I started researching and experimenting with different ways to boost my mood before I sat down to visualize my dream life. What a difference it made! So, I gathered together thirty of the best ways to raise your vibration and match the frequency of everything you want to manifest into your life, and have fun at the same time! This no-nonsense, no filler book will elevate your mood and put you on track to attract everything you want. Use any of these strategies to create your best life while improving how you feel on a daily basis.

Buy That Secret Feeling and begin to manifest your best life today. Everything you could possibly want is already on its way. You just need to feel it!

That Secret Love: 30 Practical Ways To Truly Love Who You Are

30 fun and engaging ways to practice self-love, the most

important thing you can do for yourself.

When most people hear the term 'self-love' they think it's selfish and ego-centric. Nothing could be further from the truth. In fact, if you want to have healthy, fulfilling relationships, enjoy life to the fullest, and just be happy in your own skin, it all starts with self-love. We need to give ourselves permission to put ourselves first and love who we are, unconditionally.

I struggled with this for the majority of my life. Who am I to love myself? With all my faults and imperfections? I was afraid to truly love myself and go after my dreams, and I never felt like I deserved the blessings in my life. Then a life crisis hit, and I was forced to take a good look at myself. What I found was that I deserve to be happy and fulfilled. So do you.

You are an amazing, incredible, unique human being. There is literally no one like you and there never has been. If you don't believe it, you need to change the way you feel about you! Self-love is easily the most important thing you can do for yourself.

So, I started researching and experimenting with various self-love techniques. What it did for me and my life is absolutely astounding. I am happier, have better relationships with all of my friends and family, and have a love for life I've never had before. This book is a collection of the thirty most effective strategies that I have found to deepen self-love. None of them take much time or money, but trying just one or two could literally change your life for the better.

That Secret Love will help you become everything you want to be in your life. If you want better relationships, to improve your overall mental health and well-being, and to simply enjoy life more, it all starts with self-love. Your journey starts here!

The Recurring Mortality Of Declan Darby

"Full of action, twists and turns, and laugh out loud moments. You won't want to miss this!"

He doesn't want to die again, but to save humanity, a few more times might just be worth it.

Declan Darby is unlike any of the residents of Lancaster Bay, the popular east coast tourist destination he calls home. He's unlike anyone you've ever met. Enslaved by a debilitating phobia of human touch resulting from a unique and painful ability, Declan chooses to spend his days surfing alone and his nights working as a burglar for hire.

When a routine heist goes horribly wrong, Declan uses his ability to save the life of a stranger and finds that the future has changed, sending him and his free-spirited buddy on a race against time to save humanity and the woman he desperately loves.

To prevent an impending disaster that he created, Declan must face his fears and confront the secret he has kept hidden for the majority of his life, even if it means dying, again.

The Recurring Mortality of Declan Darby is a pulse-pounding action thriller. If you like edge-of-your-seat action, twists and turns, and laugh out loud moments, then you'll love Chris Cavanagh's apocalyptic page turner.

Buy The Recurring Mortality of Declan Darby today!

★★★★★ A thrilling rollercoaster read
"The premise of this book is unlike anything I have ever encountered. The plot was a thrilling roller coaster ride of twists and turns. I love the characters. It made me laugh. It made me cry.

It has every element of a fantastic book." ~ Goodreads Reviewer

Printed in Great Britain
by Amazon

27938738R00069